Writing Strategies

Second Edition

The types of essays covered in the two Writing Strategies books are:

Book One	Book Two
Description	Process
Narration	Cause and Effect
Exposition	Extended Definition
Comparison and Contrast	Argumentation
Expository Essay with a Source	Essay with a Source and Mixed-Mode Essay

Writing Strategies

A Student-Centered Approach

Book Two: Advanced

Second Edition

David Kehe
and Peggy Dustin Kehe

PRO LINGUA ⬤ ASSOCIATES

Pro Lingua Associates, Publishers
74 Cotton Mill Hill, Suite A315
Brattleboro, Vermont 05301 USA
Office: 802 257 7779
Orders: 800 366 4775
Email: info@ProLinguaAssociates.com
        orders@ProLinguaAssociates.com
SAN: 216-0579
Webstore: www.ProLinguaAssociates.com

At ***Pro Lingua***
our objective is to foster
an approach to learning and teaching
*that we call **interplay**, the **inter**action of language*
learners and teachers with their materials,
with the language and culture,
and with each other in active, creative,
*and productive **play**.*

Copyright © 2003, 2006, 2010, 2012, 2018 by David Kehe and Peggy Dustin Kehe

ISBN 0-86647-431-5; 978-0-86647-431-3

Writing Strategies was designed by Arthur A. Burrows. It was set in Adobe Times, a digital font based on Times New Roman, at present one of the most popular type faces. Being consistent in weight and color, with sharp neoclassical serifs, it is easy to read even when set small or printed badly. Its bold is bold and its italic legible. Times New Roman is an early Twentieth Century type developed either by Victor Lardent in London in 1931 or by Starling Burgess in the United States in 1904 – there is historical controversy. No matter who drew the original Times New Roman, it was drawn from classical Roman fonts initially popular in the 1700's because they adapted well for setting Greek. The same characteristics have made it the most common modern type for phonetic alphabets and multilingual texts. This book was printed and bound by Gasch Printing in Odenton, Maryland.

Many of the photographs in this book are from Dreamstime.com: p 6 © Monkey Business Images, p 18 © Santiago Nunez Iniguez, p 33 © photographerlondon, p. 34 © Tom Wang, p 38 © Kelpfish, p 64 © Pumbal1, p 88 © Nanditha Rao, p 110 © Littleny, p 116 © Ocusfocus, p 203 © Dmires, p 204 © Shannon Fagan. The cother artwork illustrating the book is from The Big Box of Art, Copyright © 2001 Hemera Technologies Inc., and Art Explosion 750,000 Images, Copyright © 1995-2000 Nova Development Corporation. Cover art: cloth © Sahathorn Nirushtook, front photo © Diego Vito Cervo, back © Eprom

The reading selections used in *Section 2: Fluency Writing* have been rewritten for this book but are based on articles from the following sources: **Removing tattoos:** "Tattoos can be an indelible pain," *Seattle Post-Intelligencer.* **Shoplifter:** "My name is Amy and I'm a shoplifter," *Seattle Post-Intelligencer.* **Internet addiction:** "Study: on-line addicts display mental illness," *Bellingham, WA, Herald;* "Study finds nearly 6% of Web users are addicted," *Seattle Post-Intelligencer, Aug. 23, 1998*; "Addiction to Internet a growing problem," *Seattle Post-Intelligencer, May, 20, 2000.* **Research about Electronic Devices and Students' Grades**: "Phone Use and Academic Performance in a Sample of U.S. College Students,"Andrew Lepp, Jacob E. Barkley, Aryn C. Karpinski, SAGE Journals,19 February 10, 2015. **Genes:** "Happiness may be decided by genes," *Denver Post, July, 16, 1996.* **Crows:** "They're back for crowing out loud," *Seattle Post-Intelligencer, July 7, 1997.* **Organ donation:** "Gift of life or a violation in death?" *Seattle Times, July 12, 1998.*

Printed in the United States of America
Second edition, third printing 2019. 6720 copies in print.

Contents

Strategies: Decide the purpose of your essay and think of some general ideas; explain why your ideas are important; make your thesis statement sound more advanced; write a dramatic introduction; make your ideas clearer by adding examples; write a clear introduction to your paragraph with a topic sentence; make your steps clearer by describing an experience; get a reaction from a classmate; improve your style by using more advanced vocabulary, combining sentences and changing beginnings of sentences

Strategies: Write advanced rather than simple ideas for a Cause and Effect Essay; consider several topics for your essay; add details to make your ideas clearer and more interesting; write an advanced-style thesis statement; make your ideas clearer with summary statements; make your style more advanced by avoiding overgeneralization; write an interesting introduction: seven types; write an interesting conclusion; make your ideas clearer with hypothetical situations; apply the strategies and improve your style; listen to a partner read your essay to you.

CONTENTS

Essay Unit 3: *Extended Definition* 62

Strategies: Give an example; explain the parts; use similar terms to compare and contrast; use negation; tell history; get a reaction from a classmate.

Essay Unit 4: *Argumentation* 88

Strategies: Use a variety of ways to support your opinion; give the other side's opinion and then explain why it is not a good argument; write an outline to organize your ideas; interview to get more support for your argument and the other side's argument; write a clear argumentation thesis statement; use an academic style; get a reaction from a classmate.

Essay Unit 5: *Essay with a Source and Mixed-Mode Essay* 109

Strategies: Strategies: Use the sandwich technique; introduce a quote and explain it deeply; use academic expressions to introduce a quote; use academic expressions to introduce an explanation of a quote; write the first paragraph of the body first; get a reaction from a peer; use a different mode in each paragraph of the body of the essay; Listen to your partner read your essay to you.

CONTENTS

SECTION 2: FLUENCY WRITING

CONTENTS

SECTION 3: GRAMMAR EXERCISES

CONTENTS

User's Guide

Writing Strategies
A Student-Centered Approach

Book Two

Introduction

The purpose of this book and its companion volume, Book One, is to help
ESL students at the pre-college, community college, and college level meet
the requirements of academic and professional writing. There is sufficient ma-
terial in the two books for two semesters of work.

There are several unique features about these materials:

• Students learn the writing strategies through an **inductive approach**. Instead
of long explanations by either the instructor or this textbook, the students
internalize the strategies by working individually through a set of exercises,
thus, the term "student-centered" in the sub-title.

• Because students do not need lectures by the instructor, the instructor is free
to spend more time working **individually** with students during the class.

• In accordance with the **process approach**, students work with samples
of a first draft (provided in the text) and then write their own. After that,
they practice specific strategies that they can use to add to, and improve, the
content in their second drafts.

• New to this second edition is the fifth essay unit. As with the first edition,
students study modes of essays in the first four units. In this new, fifth unit,
students are introduced to using some **information from a source** in an
expository essay.

There are three sections in each of the two books. Each section features
a different aspect of writing skills development. The sections are Essays,
Fluency Writing, and Grammar.

SECTION 1: ESSAYS

Essays are the focus of the first and basic section of each book. Most writing skills texts focus on these modes. Those covered in the two books are:

Book One	**Book Two**
Description	Process
Narration	Cause and Effect
Exposition	Extended Definition
Comparison and Contrast	Argumentation
Expository Essay with a Source	Essay with a Source and Mixed-Mode Essay

SECTION 2: FLUENCY WRITING

The **Fluency Writing** section engages the students in a structured alternative to free writing or journal writing. Each activity involves pairs or triads of students in cooperative speaking, listening, and reading work with an article about real-world topics. In the final step of each activity, the students write paragraphs with the details of the article without looking at it. This requires them to make active use of the new vocabulary and sentence styles they have just worked with.

SECTION 3: GRAMMAR

The **Grammar** section is a series of activities that focus on grammatical terminology and grammatical problems typically encountered by intermediate and advanced-level students as they develop their skill in accurate and proficient composition. There are two types of activities — one type involves the students working individually on a grammar problem. The other involves groups of three students working together on problems.

The three sections can be used in a variety of ways, but a recommended procedure is to use the Essay section as the basis, proceeding step-by-step through the five units. The Fluency Writing is done at any time during the course when there is a natural break during the work on the Essays. The Grammar activities can also be done at any time when it is apparent that they are needed although there are suggestions throughout the Essay units for using these activities. Used together, the three sections of the book provide challenge and variety to the students while allowing the teacher time to work one-on-one with the students.

WRITING STRATEGIES

Each "Essay Unit" is composed of strategies that students can use when writing their essays. Some strategies are specific for a particular type of essay, but others are more generic, which means that they can be used for almost any type of essay. Thus, if an instructor decides to skip an Essay Unit, these generic strategies from that unit could still be assigned for students to practice and apply to future essays in general.

Generic strategies from Essay Unit 1: Process, that could be used with other essays:

- p. 13   Make your thesis statement sound more advanced.
- p. 16   Write a dramatic introduction.
- p. 20   Make your ideas clearer by giving examples.
- p. 22   Write a clear introduction to your paragraph with a topic sentence.
- p. 26   Get a reaction from a classmate, first and second draft (peer editing).
- p. 28   Get a reaction from a classmate, final draft (peer editing).
- p. 29   Improve your sentence style using more advanced vocabulary, combining sentences and changing the beginnings of sentences.

Generic strategies from Essay Unit 2: Cause and Effect, that could be used with other essays:

- p. 39   Add details to make your ideas clearer and more interesting.
- p. 43   Write an advanced-style thesis statement.
- p. 46   Make your ideas clearer with summary statements.
- p. 48   Make your style more advanced by avoiding overgeneralizations.
- p. 50   Write an interesting introduction (seven techniques).
- p. 53   Write an interesting conclusion (five techniques).
- p. 57   Make your ideas clearer with hypothetical situations.
- p. 61   Listen to your partner read your essay to you (peer editing).

Generic strategies from Essay Unit 3:, Extended Definition, that could be used with other essays:

- p. 80   Use a variety of sentence styles.

Generic strategies from Essay Unit 4: Argumentation, that could be used with other essays:

- p. 106   Use an academic style.

Generic strategies from Essay Unit 5: Essay with a Source and Mixed-Mode Essay, that could be used with other essays:

- p. 109   Use sources or mixed modes.

Writing Strategies

Section 1: **Essays**

Essay Unit 1: Process

(A process essay describes the sequence of steps that are followed to accomplish something.)

> *Fluency Writing:* Before starting this unit, do a Fluency Writing from Section 2, pages 132-159. After finishing, begin working individually on the following exercises.

Part 1: *Focusing on the unique features*

Transitional Expressions for Process Essays

• To begin with,	• Next,	• At this point,	• Last,
• First,	• Second,	• Right after this,	• At last,
• The first step is to	• In the third step, . . .	• Afterwards,	• Finally,
	• Meanwhile,	• After . . .	

Exercise 1: <u>Underline</u> the transitional expressions.

1.   There are some steps we should follow when training a dog. <u>To begin with</u>, we need to get the dog's attention. Next, the commands should be given clearly. Right after the dog obeys, it is vital that we reward the dog so that it will want to perform that action again in the future.

2.   When people catch colds, there is an effective process that they can follow to get better. The first step that they should take is to get warm by putting on more clothes or turning up the heat. The second is to drink a lot of liquids in order to flush out the sickness. Last, they need to rest because this will help the body build up strength to fight the virus.

3.   Taking a trip to an underdeveloped country can be a positive experience for travelers who are well prepared. First, they should get as much information as possible about the weather in that country in order to avoid a rainy season or hot season. After reading this information, they can choose the best time of year to travel and the best clothes to pack. The third step is to make preparations, if necessary, for shots and clean drinking water.

4.   As young people begin their first jobs, they are expected to be able to control their emotions, especially anger. As a child, my sister had many angry outbursts, so she had to develop a way of controlling her temper. The first step that she should follow in order to control her temper is to count to ten silently whenever she starts to feel anger. Meanwhile, she tries to imagine a pleasant scene in her mind, for example, a gently-flowing river. Afterwards, she breathes deeply and smiles.

Avoiding "you" and imperatives to improve academic style

When using an academic style, avoid the word "you" as the subject of sentences and avoid imperatives (commands, such as, *Go* to the door. *Sit* on the chair).

Possible subjects in Process Essays (to avoid "you")

- we
- they
- she or he
- it
- one
- a person
- people
- students
- parents
- children
- my friend
- a passenger
- the patient
- employees
- customers

Topic	Not Academic Style	Academic Style
How to sleep well	First, **you** should make sure **your** room is dark.	First, **we** should make sure **our** room is dark.
How to use computers	At this point, **turn on** the computer. *	At this point, **the students** can turn on **their** computers.
How to get a driver's license	After **you** pass the written test, **you** will need to take the eye exam.	After **the person** passes the written test, **she or he** will need to take the eye exam.
How to skydive from a plane	**Do** leg exercises every day.*	**My friend, Bill,** wanted to skydive, so **he** did leg exercises every day.

* The verb form in these sentences is imperative.

Exercise 2

❶ Write **Academic** next to three sentences that use an academic style.

❷ Write **Not Academic** next to four sentences that do not use an academic style.

Not Academic 1. After buying apples, you should wash them before eating them.

Academic 2. After buying apples, it is important to wash them before eating them.

_____ 3. After getting a gift, the receiver should express their appreciation.

_____ 4. Several weeks before the wedding, you should try on the wedding clothes.

_____ 5. Ann liked the feel of the keyboard of the computer, so the next step was to try out the mouse. She did this for a few minutes.

_____ 6. Your children need to know exactly what is expected of them, so give them specific instructions.

_____ 7. Carefully read all the directions first. Don't start writing until the examiner says to begin.

Exercise 3

These sentences are <u>not</u> in academic style. Re-write them by changing them to academic style.

1. (*how to be safe in a plane*) The stewardess will show you where to sit. At this point, you should buckle your seat belt.

_____

_____

2. (*how to buy a car*) Afterwards, drive the car on an expressway in order to see how it handles at high speeds.

_____

_____

3. (*how to discipline a child*) To begin with, you need to let your child explain why he thinks he got a bad math score.

_____

_____

4. (*how to climb a tall mountain*) The third step for you to take is to learn how to walk on steep, snowy slopes. You should have an ice pick to help you.

_____

_____

5. (*how to avoid divorce*) At this point, if your spouse refuses to visit a counselor with you, then you should consider going alone.

_____

_____

Exercise 4

❶ Choose four of the paragraph topics below.
❷ For those four topics, write paragraphs like those in *Exercise 1* on page 3.
❸ Use **transitional expressions** from page 3 to connect ideas.
❹ To improve **academic style**, <u>don't</u> use "you" or imperatives.
❺ Write three steps for each topic.

Example: Explain how to choose a good restaurant.

In choosing a good restaurant to go to with friends, it's important to follow this process. First, we should consider the atmosphere. It should seem informal enough so that we won't be afraid to be a little noisy. After this, if the atmosphere is appealing, we need to look at the menu to make sure that it has something for everyone's taste. Finally, the prices should be studied carefully so that we can afford to pay the bill.

Paragraph Topics

1. Explain how to lose weight.
2. Explain how to quit smoking.
3. Explain how to convince a policeman not to give a driver a speeding ticket.
4. Explain how to get a boss to give a pay raise.
5. Explain how to _____.
   (You decide.)

Grammar: *For practice with* **Comma Splices, Run-ons & Fragments**, *do Grammar Unit 1 in Section 3.*

Process Essays should be in chronological order.

Exercise 5

❶ Write **Chron** next to the four topics that have chronological order.
❷ Write **Not Chron** next to the two topics that do not have chronological order.

Chron _____ ***Topic A:*** How to make a cup of tea.
1. Boil some water.
2. Pour the boiling water over some tea leaves.
3. Wait five minutes before drinking.

_____ ***Topic B:*** How to teach a dog to retrieve a ball.
1. Tell the dog to sit and show him the ball.
2. Throw the ball and tell him to get it.
3. When he returns, give him a treat.

_____ ***Topic C:*** How to get good grades in a course.
1. Go to class every day.
2. Underline important details in the text.
3. Talk to the instructor.

_____ ***Topic D:*** How to get good grades in a course.
1. During the lecture, take notes.
2. After the lecture, ask the teacher about difficult parts.
3. Review the notes before the next class.

_____ ***Topic E:*** How to get a good job.
1. Find a job ad in the "Help Wanted" section of a newspaper.
2. Call the company and arrange an interview.
3. Go to the interview early.

_____ ***Topic F:*** How to cure a cold.
1. Wash hands often.
2. Take some vitamin C.
3. Do not do physical exercise.

Exercise 6

❶ Think of a process topic.
❷ Write three steps in chronological order.

Grammar: *For practice with **Subjects and Verbs**, do Grammar Unit 2 in Section 3.*

Grammar: *For practice with **Conjunctions**, do Grammar Unit 3 in Section 3.*

Essay: *Process* • **Part 1:** *Focusing on the unique features* • 7

Part 2: *Writing the first draft*

☞ **Preparing to write the first draft**

Exercise 7

❶ Read the first draft of the sample essay, "How to Overcome the Winter-Time Blues."

❷ Fill in the words for the list of main ideas on page 9.

Note: This is a first draft, so it is short and simple, and it may have some grammar mistakes.

Sample Essay:
(first draft)

How to Overcome the Winter-Time Blues
(first draft)

¹ Phidi is an Indonesian student studying in Minnesota. There are some steps that he could follow in order to stay cheery on cold winter days.

² To begin with, when he wakes up in the morning, he should eat breakfast because his stomach is probably empty. Eating will help keep his energy level high. If he doesn't eat breakfast, he will probably begin feeling tired and moody by noon.

³ Second, in the early afternoon, Phidi may begin to feel a little "down" so he should eat a bit of chocolate. The chocolate releases endorphins. Endorphins are natural pain-killing chemicals. However, he should eat only a little. Some people who eat too much will feel depressed later about the extra calories that they ate. So, he should choose low-fat forms. Hot chocolate can be low-fat.

⁴ Right after his last class, Phidi should be sure to get some exercise. This can raise his spirits. Walking is good for this. Of course, doing any kind of sport is a good idea, but most people can go for a walk almost anytime or anywhere, and it doesn't cost money. Any kind of exercise is helpful.

⁵ At last, in the evening, when he is studying or relaxing, Phidi should try to have lights, good smells, and music in his room. Research shows that light, even from a regular electric lamp, can improve one's mood. Also, Phidi should decide which smells he likes and buy a scented candle or cologne. If he is sad, he should light a candle and put on the cologne. In addition, he should listen to music. It can cheer him up.

⁶ In sum, people who live in a place where they get winter weather should realize that it is possible to stay happy, even on dark days. They should follow the steps described above.

How to Overcome the Winter-Time Blues

Working thesis statement:

In this essay, I will explain the steps we should take in order to overcome the winter blues.

List of main ideas

1. In morning, e _at_____ br_____ to keep energy high.
2. In early afternoon, eat ch_____.
    a. Chocolate releases en_____.
    b. Choose lo_____ - fa_____ hot chocolate.
3. After classes, get ex_____ to raise sp_____.
4. In evening, have li_____, good sm_____ and m_____.
    a. Regular electric la_____.
    b. Scented ca_____ or co_____.

☞ First draft assignment

Exercise 8

Choose a topic from below. (**Note:** Choose a topic that you will not be embarrassed to have a classmate read about. Later, a classmate will read your essay.)

Process Essay Topic Choices

Explain how to . . .

- choose a university to attend.

- relieve stress before a test.

- have a perfect date with someone.

- catch a criminal (i.e. someone who committed a crime).

- break up with a boyfriend/girlfriend but still remain friendly.

- pass a test or course without studying.

- convince a teacher to pass you in a course that you have done poorly in.

- impress someone on a first date.

- form a music band.

- plan a trip with a friend.

- get your parents to do what you want them to do, or to agree with your ideas.

- Other topic: Tell your teacher <u>before</u> starting the essay.

Strategy 1   Decide the purpose of your essay and think of some general ideas.

Exercise 9

Write a **Working Thesis Statement** and **List of Main Ideas**. *(See samples on page 9.)*

Types of *Working Thesis Statements* *(Choose one.)*

- In this paper, I will discuss / explain / describe . . .
- This paper will focus on . . .
- This paper will discuss / describe
- The purpose of this paper is to discuss / explain / describe . . .

Chart

Working thesis statement: _____

_____

_____

List of main ideas: (You should have *more than two* main ideas.)

Remember: *Your essay must be in* **chronological order**. *(See sample on page 7.)*

Grammar: *For practice with* **Prepositional Phrases** and **Prepositions,** *do Grammar Unit 3 and Grammar Unit 4.*

☛ First draft assignment — Write the first draft

Exercise 10: Write a first draft of a ***Process Essay*** with the main ideas and some details. *(See sample on page 8.)*

Grammar: *For practice with* **Independent and Dependent Clauses,** *do Grammar Unit 6.*

Part 3: *Writing the second draft*

☛ Preparing to write the second draft

(Think about improving your first draft while you do these exercises.)

Strategy 2	Explain why your ideas are important.

Expressions for explaining reasons for <u>one</u> step

• so   • in order to   • because   • By doing this,

Exercise 11

❶ Write **Good** if the paragraph explains the reason for <u>one step</u> in the process.
❷ Write **Not Good** if:
     a. the paragraph explains more than one step in the process, or
     b. it does not explain the reasons for that one step in the process.
❸ If it is not correct, explain the reason why it is not correct.

1. *Topic:* Explain how to choose a good movie to watch.

> Often, we don't want to waste our time watching a bad movie. Therefore, we should first ask our friends to recommend a movie. Next, it's a good idea to look in the newspaper to see where the movie is playing.

Not Good   **Reason:** *This does not explain only one step in the process* .

2. *Topic:* Explain how to choose a good movie to watch.

> Often, we don't want to waste our time watching a bad movie. Therefore, we should first ask our friends to recommend a movie. Usually, our friends know our taste in movies, so they are likely to know what type we would like to see.

Good   **Reason:** _____ .

3. *Topic:* Explain how to write a novel.

> Of course, the novelist wants to write a book that will be popular. Therefore, the first step is to watch the most popular TV programs for a week. By doing this, the writer will quickly learn what topics potential readers are interested in.

Good   **Reason:** _____ .

4. *Topic:* Explain how to write a novel.

> Of course, the novelist wants to write a book that will be popular. Therefore, the first step is to watch the most popular TV programs for a week. By doing this, the writer can write a novel.

Not Good   **Reason:** *This does not explain the reason for that one step.* .

5. *Topic:* Explain how to bargain for a good price for a car.

The customer should never smile while looking at the car. In fact, the first thing that they should do is to have a serious look on their face. Next, they should look at the price tag for the car. Finally, telling the salesman that they are just looking, rather than buying, is helpful. These steps can be effective in order to bargain for a good price.

_____**Reason:** _____

6. *Topic:* Explain how to bargain for a good price for a car.

The customer should never smile while looking at the car. In fact, the first thing that they should do is to have a serious look on their face in order to give the impression that they have a lot of experience with car-shopping.

_____**Reason:** _____.

7. *Topic:* Explain how to drive safely on an expressway.

After drivers have successfully entered the expressway, they may want to pass slower-moving cars in their lane. Before changing lanes, they should turn their heads to the left so they can drive safely on the expressway.

_____**Reason:** _____.

8. *Topic:* Explain how to drive safely on an expressway.

After drivers have successfully entered the expressway, they may want to pass slower-moving cars in their lane. Before changing lanes, they should turn their heads to the left so they can see if there are any cars next to them.

_____**Reason:** _____.

9. *Topic:* Explain how to improve one's personality.

My brother would like to have more friends but seems to have problems because he is shy. To overcome his shyness, he should first try to just say something brief to a stranger (for example, a sales clerk) because he needs to develop the habit of speaking.

_____**Reason:** _____.

10. *Topic:* Explain how to improve one's personality.

My brother would like to have more friends but seems to have some problems because he is shy. To overcome his shyness, he should first try to just say something brief to a stranger (for example, a sales clerk). By doing this, he can improve his personality.

_____**Reason:** _____.

Exercise 12

❶ Choose <u>three</u> of the topics below.

❷ Write paragraphs like those in *Exercise 11* *(page 11)*. Describe **just one step** in a process and **explain the reason** for that one step.

❸ Use one of the **Expressions for Explaining Reasons** *(page 11)* in order to explain the reason for the step, and <u>underline</u> it.

❹ Use **Academic Style** [In other words, do not use "you" or imperatives (i.e. commands)].

Example: **Topic**: <u>Explain how to improve our eyesight.</u>

Step: <u>Blink the eyes quickly</u>

After doing the focusing exercise, we are ready to do "fast blinking." In this step, we blink our eyes quickly for five seconds, stop blinking for five seconds, and then repeat this routine for one minute. <u>By doing this</u>, we will create moisture which contains nutrients. These nutrients help maintain a healthy eyeball.

---

1. **Topic:** Explain how to stay awake until 4 a.m.

2. **Topic:** Explain how to take a good picture with a smartphone.

3. **Topic:** Explain how to stop smoking.

4. **Topic:** Explain how to get an autograph from a famous person.

5. **Topic:** Explain how to make a great website.

6. **Topic:** Explain how to choose a computer.

7. **Topic:** (You decide a topic.)

Strategy 3   Make your thesis statement sound more advanced.

- **A Working Thesis Statement** in the introduction of the first draft helps writers start writing and get focused as they begin to think of ideas for their essay.

- **An Advanced-style Thesis Statement** can be better in the introduction of the <u>final draft</u> of an essay.

Exercise 13

Fill in the blanks with the correct **Advanced-style Thesis Statements** from the box. As you use the statements, check them off, as we have done with the third statement.

Advanced-style Thesis Statements

___ In fact, there are some important reasons why exercising in the afternoon is best for our health.

___ There are several valuable lessons that children can learn by visiting a zoo.

_X_ A student who is interested in meeting new people at college may want to follow these steps to achieve an active social life.

___ A person's relationship with family members and co-workers can suffer if the person works more than 50 hours a week, as the following examples of negative effects illustrate.

---

1. *Topic:* Meeting new people

   Working Thesis Statement *(in the first draft)*: In this essay, I will explain some steps that a student can take in order to meet new people at college.

   Advanced-style Thesis Statement *(in the final draft)*: *A student who is interested in meeting new people at college may want to follow these steps to achieve an*

2. *Topic:* Reasons for visiting a zoo

   Working Thesis Statement *(in the first draft)*: This essay will focus on several valuable lessons that children can learn by visiting a zoo.

   Advanced-style Thesis Statement: _____

   _____

3. *Topic:* What is the best time of day to exercise?

   Working Thesis Statement *(in the first draft)*: The purpose of this essay is to explain why it is better for our health to exercise in the afternoon.

   Advanced-style Thesis Statement: _____

   _____

4. *Topic:* Effects of working more than 50 hours a week

   Working Thesis Statement *(in the first draft)*: This paper will discuss the negative effects that working more than 50 hours a week can have on a person's relationship with family members and co-workers.

   Advanced-style Thesis Statement: _____

   _____

   _____

Exercise 14

Write an **Advanced-style Thesis Statement** for each.

1. *Topic:* Family relationships

   Working Thesis *(in the first draft)*: The purpose of this paper is to describe some ways in which parents can improve their relationship with teenage children.
   Advanced-style Thesis *(in the final draft)*: _____
   _____

2. *Topic:* Do you think money is important for happiness?

   Working Thesis *(in the first draft)*: In this essay, I will explain the reasons why I feel that people in the middle class are happier than very wealthy people.
   Advanced-style Thesis: _____
   _____

3. *Topic:* The effects of the Internet

   Working Thesis *(in the first draft):* This paper will focus on the effects the Internet has on college students' education.
   Advanced-style Thesis: _____
   _____

Common Grammatical Mistakes with Process Thesis Statements

- **Mistake**: There are several <u>steps how</u> to build a snowman.
- **Correct** : There are several <u>steps that we can follow </u>to build a snowman.

- **Mistake**: These are <u>steps how</u> to choose a good video to watch.
- **Correct** : These are <u>steps that one should follow in order to</u> choose a good video to watch.

Exercise 15

❶ Write **Right** next to the <u>two thesis statements</u> that are good.
❷ Write **Wrong** next to the <u>two thesis statements</u> that are grammatically weak.

_____ 1. There are a few steps how to improve our eyesight.

_____ 2. There are several steps that people can follow in order to prepare their houses for winter.

_____ 3. In order to have a successful dinner party, the host and hostess should follow these steps.

_____ 4. These are steps how to become a great video game player.

Exercise 16

Rewrite the two thesis statements in Exercise 15 above that are grammatically weak.

Strategy 4   Write a dramatic introduction.

Writing a Dramatic Introduction

A dramatic introduction has some special features:

◊ It has action.
◊ It happens during one day.
◊ It has two paragraphs.

• The first paragraph tells a *very short story* about what happened during one day.
• The second paragraph explains how the story is connected to your topic.
  The last sentence is usually the *thesis statement*.

Example

Essay topic: *Traveling by train is better than by plane.*

Explanation	Essay
The essay starts with a story. *The story has action.*	Dan nervously flipped through a magazine as he waited for the other passengers to get into their seats. Soon, a very large man sat down in the seat next to him. His shoulders were so wide that they pushed Dan's elbow off the arm rest. The take-off and first 20 minutes were smooth. Dan lowered the tray in front of him and set his lunch and coffee on it. Suddenly, the passenger in front of him decided to push her seat back, shoving Dan's tray into him, spilling coffee all over him. For the rest of the two-hour flight, he tried not to think about how miserable he felt in his tiny seat and wet shirt.
The second paragraph shows connection to topic. Last sentence is thesis statement.	Most people, at some time, need to travel a long distance for business or pleasure. Unfortunately, many of them consider traveling only by plane and forget that going by train is an option. In fact, going somewhere by train is much better than by plane.

Exercise 17

Two of the introductions below are good dramatic introductions. The others are not good dramatic introductions. Describe the good or weak points of each introduction on the line below it. Use the descriptions in this box:

Introduction Descriptions

☐ Good dramatic introduction.
☐ Good dramatic introduction.
☐ Weak: There is little action.
☑ Weak: There is no story in the introduction.
☐ Weak: It does not happen during one day.
☐ Weak: There is a story but not two paragraphs.
☐ Weak: The second paragraph continues the story.
☐ Weak: The first paragraph is a story but the first sentence does not start the story.

Topic: All families should have pets.

1. A famous person once said, "A dog is the only thing in the world that will love you more than you love yourself." Most people would agree that this world needs more love, and pets, not just dogs, are able to provide that. In fact, a dog can have an interesting effect on a family.

"Introduction Description" from the box above: *Weak: There is no story in the introduction.*

2. One day, 9-year-old Timmy got a puppy. That morning, he took the puppy, named Rex, to the back yard and tried to train him. Pushing Rex's rear, Timmy told him to sit. After Rex sat, he gave him a treat. Next, he wanted to teach him to chase a ball. However, every time Timmy threw the ball, Rex grabbed it and ran away from Timmy. Soon, Timmy gave up and went inside to play video games.

   Pets require a lot of attention and patience. Unfortunately, today many children, like Timmy, lack both. By giving children the responsibility for training a pet, parents can help them learn some important lessons for life. In fact, there are steps that a child can follow in order to train a dog.

"Introduction Description" from the box above: _____

3. Cats are often difficult to train. One evening, I decided to try a new technique. About an hour before going to bed, I started to play with her. I got her to chase a ball of string. Also, I put a big paper bag on the floor, which she loved to play inside of. After an hour, we were both tired and slept through the night.

   Other pet owners could probably learn from my experience with my cat. It is clear that pet owners have to use their own brains when training pets. This is just one reason why it is important for families to have pets.

"Introduction Description" from the box above: _____

4. One day, Ann bought a dog. That night, something bad happened, and the dog saved Ann's life. She was glad that she had a dog to protect her.

There are a number of good points about owning a dog. Anyone who is interested in getting a dog may want to follow this process in order to find one that has the appropriate characteristics.

"Introduction Description" from the box above: _____

5. It was about 2 a.m. All the family members were sleeping upstairs in their beds. Suddenly, their dog, Winnie, came upstairs and started barking, but nobody woke up. Next, he went inside the parents' bedroom and jumped up on the bed. The father got up, and Winnie ran to the hallway. Following Winnie, the father noticed smoke coming from downstairs.

The father went down the steps and saw that a fire had started in the living room. He ran upstairs, got his wife and children, and everyone ran outside. Winnie had saved their lives. This is one reason why it's important for all families to own a pet.

"Introduction Description" from the box above: _____

6. When Sara returned home from school, she started to feed her goldfish, as she always did. However, today she noticed that one of the fish was floating on its side on top of the water. She called her mother, who explained to Sara that the fish had died. After removing the fish and burying it in the backyard, the family had a long talk about the cycle of life.

"Introduction Description" from the box above: _____

7. This morning, George got up and ate his breakfast alone, just as he has done for the past years since his wife died. After breakfast, he put a leash on his dog, Callie, and walked her to the park. As they were walking, a young woman on the sidewalk stopped and asked if she could pet Callie. They had a short, pleasant conversation about the dog. When they reached the park, another dog ran up to Callie, and that dog's owner soon arrived. While the two dogs played together, George and the other owner had an interesting discussion about the news of that day.

Pets can be advantageous for their owners. In George's case, his dog, Callie, helped him meet new people. In fact, pet dogs provide a variety of physical, social and emotional benefits.

"Introduction Description" from the box above: _____

8.   Hong recently moved into a new neighborhood. Although it seemed nice, she was a little worried because she lived alone, so she bought a dog. After a week, she started to feel secure in her new home, but one night she heard someone trying to open her back door. Her dog, Rusty, started to bark near the door, and soon the person left. The next morning, Hong noticed some police cars in front of her neighbor's house She found out that someone had broken into that house, tied up the owners and robbed them!

Most people know that a dog can provide some protection against crime. However, there are limitations about a dog's ability to help In order to make a home truly secure, there are several steps that a home-owner can take.

"Introduction Description" from the box above: _____

Exercise 18

1) Choose two of the topics from the box below.
2) Write a two-paragraph dramatic introduction for each.
3) Underline the thesis statement.
4) Do not write the complete essay. Write only the introductions.

Topic Choices

Explain . . .

- how an older person can look younger.

- how to convince a policeman not to give us a ticket.

- how to make new friends at school.

- the effects that social media have on young people.

- what causes a family to have close relationships.

- what causes video games to be so popular.

- which is better: living alone or with a roommate.

- whether high school students should wear uniforms.

- whether spanking is the best way to discipline a child.

Section 1: Essays • Essay 1: Process

| **Strategy 5** | Make your ideas clearer by giving examples. |

Exercise 19

Write the correct topic from the box for each paragraph below.

Topics:
_____ how to prepare for a marathon
_____ how to impress an employer
_____ how to choose a pet dog

1. *Topic:* _____

The buyer needs to decide what size dog will be best for their family. **For example,** if the buyer lives in a small apartment, a terrier would be a good choice. On the other hand, a retriever would fit well with a family who has a large yard.

2. *Topic:* _____

The night before the race, runners should eat a dinner that will give them stamina the next day. **For instance,** my brother, who is a marathon runner, eats spaghetti before a race because the carbohydrates provide him with energy over several hours.

3. *Topic:* _____

Workers can do some extra tasks that other workers avoid. **For example,** they could clean up the lunch room and wash dirty coffee cups after other workers leave.

Exercise 20

Add an example for each of the sentences below like those in Exercise 19 above.

1. *how to get a good grade in this class*

The students need to have good study habits. **For example,** _____
_____

2. *how to overcome shyness*

Next, it is helpful for shy people to attend a party. To prepare for the event, they should practice ways to start a conversation with a stranger. **For instance,** _____

_____

3. *how to stay healthy in old age*

In addition to exercising their bodies, it is important for elderly people to exercise their minds. **For example,** _____

_____

Exercise 21

❶ Think of <u>two topics</u>.

❷ Write paragraphs like those in Exercises 19 & 20 above. Write a sentence and give an example. (You can use any of the topics in this unit, e.g. on pp. 13 and 19.)

Grammar: *For practice with* **Noun Clauses***, do Grammar Unit 8.*

| Strategy 6 | Write a clear introduction to your paragraph with a topic sentence. |

Exercise 22

Fill in the blanks with the correct topic sentences from the box.

_____ Because it is common for students to carry backpacks to school these days, they should follow these tips in order to avoid back problems.

_____ In order to help relieve stress at work, some companies allow pets in the offices.

_____ One way in which some people try to get money illegally is by cheating an insurance company.

---

1. _____
_____. During breaks, employees can play with the pets or take them for a walk. Research has shown that spending time with animals can lower a person's blood pressure and greatly reduce tension.

2. _____
_____. First, they should choose one with a waist strap which will distribute weight evenly. Second, the load in the backpack should not exceed 15% of their body weight. Finally, they should use both shoulder straps.

3. _____
_____. An example of this happened recently. A man who had lost $250,000 by gambling bought an insurance policy that would pay him $1.5 million if he became disabled. Then, he hired a friend to cut off his foot in order to collect the money. He told the police and insurance company that he lost his foot as a result of an accident. However, investigators were able to uncover his scheme.

Exercise 23

❶ Write **Good** next to the three paragraphs that have a good topic sentence.
❷ Write **Not Good** next to the three paragraphs that do not have a good topic sentence.
❸ Underline the good topic sentences.

_____ 1. Most people would agree that on a small campus, the crime rate is lower than on a large one. In addition, smaller colleges tend to give students more individual support in their educational needs. For example, instructors usually have more time to help students after class.

_____ 2. There are problems with the early closing time of the computer lab on campus. Many students have classes until 8 p.m., so they are unable to get to the computer labs before the 9 p.m. closing time. Furthermore, during the afternoon, all the computers in the lab are occupied, which means there are students who would probably use them later at night if they could. Some students, like me, prefer to use the computer lab after 10 p.m., when all my other studies are finished.

_____ 3. There are two techniques that we can follow in order to develop a better relationship with our boss. First, we can keep our boss informed. If we notice a problem that our boss is not aware of, we should tell them about it. Next, we can compliment our boss. Usually, our boss has a supervisor. When we get a chance, we should say something nice about our boss to the supervisor.

_____ 4. It's a good idea to bring small toys or books for children to read on the plane. Also, the parents should bring plenty of snacks since the children may not be able to wait for the food service on the flight. Taking a flight late at night may be wise because the child will probably sleep most of the time.

_____ 5. In 1946, 74% of the people said that spanking children was a good form of discipline. However, in 1997, only 66% felt it was acceptable. In addition, in both years, more than 80% said that, as children, they were spanked.

_____ 6. Surprisingly, gang members who join the army make great soldiers, according to research. They understand how to follow a leader, and they are not afraid of anything. Also, they are very loyal to their group.

Exercise 24

Write topic sentences for these paragraphs.

1. _____
_____. First, they should arrive at the airport early. Also, they should not fly on an empty stomach, but they should not drink caffeine and alcohol, either. When they start to feel nervous, they should try to relax by using deep breathing techniques. Finally, they should avoid reading newspaper articles about airline accidents.

2. _____
_____. In America, coffee houses are the busiest in the mornings. In Japan, the busy times are in the afternoons and evenings. Americans drink coffee as a way to get energy. However, in Japan, it is used as a way to socialize.

3. _____
_____. My older brother, Tom, is an
extrovert. On the weekends, he is usually out with his friends. In high school, he
belonged to several clubs because he enjoyed being around people. Ken, my younger
brother, is the opposite. He prefers to spend time alone hiking or reading. When he
goes to a party, he usually talks with just one or two people.

4. _____
_____. For example, after watching
popular TV programs about young people, some teenagers may feel disappointed if they
do not have a lot of funny and interesting friends like the characters on the TV shows
have. Also, they might begin to feel depressed if they do not have close family members,
beautiful clothes, or a huge house, similar to what they see on TV.

Exercise 25

   ❶ Write a paragraph with a topic sentence and some details.
   ❷ <u>Underline</u> the topic sentences.

Strategy 7   Make your steps clearer by describing an experience.

Exercise 26

    Fill in the blanks with the correct words from the box.

_____ she takes a break		_____ My roommate	
_____ Tom's expensive boat		_____ During the office visit,	
_____ were on the computer		_____ For example, Mary	
_____ interested in her job		_____ he underlined	
_____ Let's say that two people, Tom and Sue,			

1. *Topic: how to get good grades in a course*
   Step: Talk to the teacher about the difficult parts of the textbook.

   The next step is to talk to the teacher after class. _____, who is an
   excellent student, was having problems understanding his psychology course. To get
   help, _____ the difficult parts in his textbook, wrote questions
   about these parts in the margins, and made an appointment to talk to his instructor in
   her office. _____, he didn't waste her time
   because he was well prepared with his questions.

2. *Topic: how to prevent a cold*
   Step: Wash hands often.

The first step in preventing a cold is to wash one's hands often, especially during the cold season. _____ works in an office, and she shares a phone and computer with two other workers. If one of Mary's officemates has a cold, after she uses the computer, _____ and washes her hands with soap and water for 15 seconds in order to wash away any germs that _____ _____ .

3. *Topic: how to avoid a divorce*
   Step: Go to a counselor.

Finally, another possible way to save the marriage is for the unhappy couple to visit a counselor. During the session with the counselor, both the wife and husband will have a chance to explain their point of view. _____ went to a counselor for help with their marriage. Tom explained to the counselor that the reason why he was dissatisfied with the marriage was because Sue was only _____ _____ and spent every weekend working. Sue, on the other hand, said that she felt pressure to work hard because they needed more money to pay for _____ .

Exercise 27

❶ Choose <u>two topics</u> from below.
❷ Write about <u>one step</u> and include your experience or another person's experience to explain the step.

Topics

Explain how to …

- lose weight.
- quit smoking.
- convince a policeman not to give a ticket.
- convince a boss to give a pay raise.
- buy a car.
- get an autograph from a famous person.
- meet new people.
- (You decide on a topic.)

- avoid stress before an exam.
- choose a pet to buy.
- choose a computer/smartphone.
- choose an apartment.
- have a good camping trip.
- make a friend on social media.
- improve our physical appearance.

Strategy 8

Part I: Get a reaction from a classmate.

Exercise 28

Read this sample essay titled "How to Overcome the Winter-Time Blues." Imagine that you have a classmate who wants your opinion about the essay.

Sample Essay:
(second draft)

How to Overcome the Winter-Time Blues

Every morning, Phidi **Δ1** gets up at 7 a.m. In summer this is easy for him, but in winter he has difficulties because it is still dark outside. When he was in Indonesia, it was warm and sunny, even on winter mornings. **Δ2** In this essay, I will describe steps that Phidi should follow in order to stay cheery on cold winter mornings. **Δ3**

To begin with, when he wakes up in the morning, he should eat breakfast because his stomach is probably empty. Eating will help keep his energy level high. If he doesn't eat breakfast, he will probably begin feeling tired and moody by noon. **Δ4**

Second, in the early afternoon, Phidi may begin to feel a little "down" **Δ5** so he should eat a bit of chocolate. The chocolate releases endorphins. Endorphins are natural pain-killing chemicals. **Δ6** However, he should eat only a little. Some people who eat too much will feel depressed later about the extra calories that they ate. So, Phidi should choose low-fat forms. The drink hot chocolate can be low-fat.

Right after his last class, Phidi should be sure to get some exercise. **Δ7** This can raise his spirits. Walking is good for this. Of course, doing any kind of sport is a good idea, but most people can go for a walk almost anytime or anywhere, and it doesn't cost money. Any kind of exercise is helpful.

At last, in the evening, when he is studying or relaxing, Phidi should try to have lights, good smells, and music in his room. **Δ 8** Research shows that light, even from a regular lamp, can improve one's mood. Also, Phidi should decide which smells he likes and buy scented candles or cologne.

In sum, people who live in a place where they get winter weather should realize that it is possible to stay happy, even on dark days. They **Δ9** follow the steps described above.

Exercise 29

Imagine that your classmate asks you these questions about the essay. Write your advice.

Example

Question

1. Look at where I wrote #1. Do you think that I should explain that Phidi is from Indonesia here? Why or why not? How can I improve it?

Advice

No, it's not necessary here because you say that in the third sentence. I like the way that you put it there.

---

2. Look at #2. Do you think that this is a good dramatic introduction? Why or why not?

3. Look at #3. I want to have an advanced-style thesis statement. How can I change it?

4. Look at #4. I'd like to include an example of a good breakfast here. What do you think he should eat for breakfast for stamina?

5. Look at #5. I think that I need a comma here. Do I write it "down," or "down", ? In other words, do I put the comma inside or outside the quotation marks?

6. Look at the sentence before #6. Do you think this information is interesting? Do you think that it is important that I include this sentence? Why?

7. Look at #7. I'd like to combine these two sentences that I underlined. How can I do it?

8. Look at #8. I'd like to include someone's experience with music here. What kind of music do you like to listen to when you are trying to relax?

9. Look at #9. Is it better to write "They follow" or "They should follow" here?

☞ Second draft assignment — Write the second draft

Exercise 30

Write a second draft of the *Process Essay* that you wrote on page 10. Try to improve your first draft by using the strategies:

- Explain why your ideas are important. *(See page 11.)*
- Make your thesis statement sound more advanced. *(See page 13.)*
- Write an interesting (dramatic) introduction. *(See page 16.)*
- Make your ideas clearer for the reader (by adding examples). *(See page 20.)*
- Introduce your paragraphs clearly. *(See page 22.)*

Also, try to use:
- transitional expressions. *(See page 3.)*
- academic style (i.e. do not use "you" or imperatives). *(See page 4.)*
- chronological order. *(See page 7.)*

Fluency Writing: While working on your second draft, do a Fluency Writing from Section 2. After finishing the Fluency Writing, continue working on your second draft.

Part 4: *Writing the final draft*

☞ Preparing to write the final draft, using peer-editing

Strategy 8   **Part II:** Get a reaction from a classmate.

Exercise 31: After you finish your second draft:

❶ Write some numbers on your second draft in places where you would like advice from another student. *(See sample on page 26.)*

❷ On a different paper, write questions that you would like to ask. *(See sample on page 27.)*

Possible questions that you might ask to get advice

- Do you think I need more details here?
- Can you understand this sentence?
- How can I combine these two sentences?
- Is this part interesting?
- Can you help me think of some details that I could use here?
- Do you think there is a grammar problem in this sentence?
- What transitional expression should I use here?

Exercise 32

Find a classmate.

❶ Exchange essays with your partner.
❷ Silently read your partner's essay.
❸ Point to the places on your essay where you would like advice and ask your questions. *(You do not have to make any changes to your essay if you do not want to.)*
❹ Also, answer your partner's questions about their essay.

(Just discuss your advice. You <u>do not have to write</u> your advice.)

Grammar: *For practice with* **Reduced Adverb Clauses**, *do Grammar Unit 9. Reduced clauses are especially useful in process essays.*

Strategy 9 Improve your sentence style by using more advanced vocabulary, combining sentences, and changing the beginnings of sentences

Exercise 33

To improve the essay "How to Overcome the Winter-Time Blues" on the next page, fill in the blanks with the correct words and phrases from the box below. These are replacements for the language in parentheses. (To see the earlier drafts of the essay, see pages 8 and 26.)

Paragraphs 1-2: ___ depressed   ___ struggling to keep   ___ drags himself
___ suffer psychologically and physically from the decreased sunlight and the cold
_X_ a freezing, gloomy
___ filled with work in classrooms, labs, and the library
Paragraphs 3-4-5: ___ some exercise in order to
___ it is recommended that he eat
___ lunchtime, he always
___ low-fat forms, such as the drink hot chocolate or a small candy bar
___ eat breakfast in order to replace the calories he burned during the previous night
___ can help relieve stress and improve one's mood
___ endorphins, which   ___ To make sure
Paragraphs 6-7:   ___ Whenever he needs to cheer himself up
___ on dark, gloomy
___ By following these steps and paying attention to their habits and environment, they
        can keep their spirits up.
___ feel happier, since it reminds
___ listening to music that he enjoys can cheer him up

Sample Essay:
(preparing the
final draft)

How to Overcome the Winter-Time Blues

¹ It is 11 a.m. on (an ugly) _____*a freezing, gloomy*_____ winter day, but Phidi, an Indonesian student studying at an American college, is (having difficulty keeping) _____ his eyes open during the lecture. He sits up straight and breathes deeply, but soon his body slouches down, his eyes slowly close and he starts to dream. At noon, he (goes) _____ back to his room and takes some medicine for the cough that he has had for the past three weeks, and he tries to take a nap. His afternoon and evening are (busy)_____ _____. At the end of the day, Phidi is (sad) _____ and he wonders if he made a mistake by leaving warm, sunny Indonesia for cold, dark Minnesota.

² Like Phidi, many people who live in cold climates (feel bad in winter) _____ _____ . However, there are some steps that they could follow in order to stay cheery on dark winter days.

³ To begin with, when Phidi wakes up in the morning, he should (eat breakfast, because his stomach is probably empty) _____ _____. Eating will help keep his energy level high. If he doesn't eat breakfast, he will probably begin feeling tired and moody by noon. An example of someone who had energy problems was my brother. (He wanted to be sure) _____that he wouldn't get tired before (lunchtime. He always) _____ ate eggs and fried potatoes and drank two glasses of milk for breakfast.

⁴ Second, in the early afternoon, Phidi may begin to feel a little "down," so (he should eat) _____ a bit of chocolate. The chocolate releases (endorphins. Endorphins) _____ are natural pain-killing chemicals. However, he should eat only a little. Some people who eat too much will feel depressed later about the extra calories that they ate. So, Phidi should choose (low-fat forms. The drink hot chocolate can be low-fat) _____ _____.

⁵ Right after his last class, Phidi should be sure to get (some exercise. This can) _____ raise his spirits. Walking is good for this. Of course, doing any kind of sport is a good idea, but almost anyone can go for a walk anytime or anywhere, even just for ten minutes, and it doesn't cost money. Any kind of exercise (is helpful) _____.

⁶ At last, in the evening, when he is studying or relaxing, Phidi should try to have lights, good smells and music in his room. Research shows that light, even from a regular electric lamp, can lift the spirits. Also, Phidi should decide which smells he likes best and buy some cologne or a scented candle. (Whenever he is sad) _____ _____, he should light a candle and put on the cologne. In addition, (he should listen to music. It can cheer him up) _____ _____. For me, the best music to listen to when I'm feeling a bit down is something with guitars. This type of music always makes me (feel happier. It reminds) _____ me of the enjoyable summer I had a few years ago when I visited Spain.

⁷ In sum, people who live in a place where they get winter weather should realize that it is possible to stay happy, even (on bad) _____ days. (They should follow these steps) _____ _____.

☛ Final draft assignment — Write the final draft

Exercise 34

Write a final draft of the *Process Essay* that you began on page 10. Try to improve the sentence style and, if you want, use some of the ideas that your peer-editing partner recommended.

Essay 2: Cause and Effect

(A cause and effect essay explains the reasons why something happened and the results.)

Fluency Writing: Before starting this unit, do a Fluency Writing from Section 2. After finishing, begin working individually on the following exercises.

Part 1: *Focusing on the unique features*

Expressions for Causes (Reasons)

- because
- since
- because of *
- For that reason,

* *Hint:* **"because of"** is a preposition:

"*Because of the rain,* I got wet." (**Mistake:** *Because of it was raining,* I got wet.)

Exercise 1

❶ Underline the <u>reason</u> and write "cause" above it.

❷ Double-underline the <u>result</u> and write "effect" above it.

1. Because <u>the traffic was heavy,</u> <u style="text-decoration: underline double">we were late for the concert.</u>
   (cause) ... *(effect)*

2. There was a large crowd attending the game because of the popularity of the superstar player.

3. She wasn't able to get to sleep since she had drunk too much coffee after dinner.

4. Because I had left my car lights on all night, the battery was dead in the morning.

5. During the race, Joe got a terrible stomachache. For that reason, he quit running at the halfway point.

Exercise 2

❶ Use the set of cue words (in parentheses).

❷ Write sentences using **expressions for causes**.

❸ Underline the <u>reason</u> and write "cause" above it.

❹ Double-underline the <u>result</u> and write "effect" above it.

1. (computer/job). *Because of his great computer skills,* *my brother was able to get a high-paying job.*
   (cause) ... *(effect)*

2. (teacher/sick/ class/ canceled)

3. (afraid to fly/ travel by train)

4. (needed a car/ borrowed money)

5. (passed an exam/ celebrated)

6. (You write a sentence.)

> ### Expressions for Effects (Results)
>
> • as a result • therefore • so • consequently

Exercise 3

❶ Underline the <u>reason</u> and write "cause" above it.
❷ Double-underline the <u>result</u> and write "effect" above it.

1. *cause*
It was raining, so *effect* my hair got wet.

2. While in Paris, Sam became fluent in French. As a result, he was able to make some French friends

3. My brother feels a lot of stress from his job. Therefore, he likes to spend time alone in the mountains on weekends.

4. The Nelsons built an extra bedroom in their house so their son could have his own room.

5. The war lasted for several years. Consequently, the economy was ruined.

Exercise 4

❶ Use the set of cue words (in parentheses).
❷ Write sentences using **expressions for effects**.
❸ Underline the <u>reason</u> and write "cause" above it.
❹ Double-underline the <u>result</u> and write "effect" above it.

1. (lift weights/big muscles) *cause* About 6 months ago, Bill started lifting weights.
effect As a result, his muscles got bigger.

2. (joined a club/met new people)

3. (stole money/prison)

4. (practiced hard/won a prize)

Exercise 5

Read the following two sample Cause and Effect Essays. Notice that they use two different organization patterns.

Sample First Drafts of Essays:

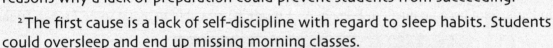

Sample 1: # Failing in College
(first draft)

[1] Going to college is an occasion for excitement and expectations. However, students who are unprepared are likely to fail. In fact, there are several reasons why a lack of preparation could prevent students from succeeding.

[2] The first cause is a lack of self-discipline with regard to sleep habits. Students could oversleep and end up missing morning classes.

[3] In addition, poor study habits are a reason why students fail. For example, some students do not know how to take good notes in lecture classes.

[4] Finally, a number of students fail because of their weak skills. Some students may know a lot about a subject, for example, Science, but are weak in a skill, such as writing. As a result, they tend to perform poorly, in general, on assignments.

[5] To sum up, many students who fail lack self-discipline, wise study habits, and/or good skills.

Sample 2: # Culture Shock *(first draft)*

[6] After arriving in a foreign country, many people feel excited about their new adventure. However, for some people, the sense of excitement soon changes to culture shock. Travelers with culture shock often experience a variety of unpleasant effects.

[7] To begin with, the traveler will feel confused. Due to the fact that the language, food and customs are different, the traveler might have problems knowing how to get information, what to eat, or even what to do.

[8] Another effect of culture shock is a loss of energy. The traveler may just want to stay in bed in order to avoid confronting any strange situations outside his room.

[9] Third, travelers with culture shock often become ill due to stress. It is not unusual for them to catch a cold or develop indigestion shortly after arriving in the foreign country.

[10] The fourth effect is the development of a bad attitude toward the new culture. In some cases, because experiences do not meet the traveler's expectations, they are apt to blame the people or unfamiliar customs for their discomfort.

[11] Travelers should be prepared to experience culture shock. If they are patient and aware of the effects of culture shock, they can usually overcome uncomfortable feelings.

Exercise 6

❶ Refer to the two sample essays on page 34 and above.

❷ Below, choose the phrases from the boxes to fill in the blanks.

Organization Pattern 1: Several causes result in one general effect.

_X_ have poor study habits		___ lack self-discipline
___ Some students are unable to succeed.		___ have weak skills

Title: *Failing in College*

Cause 1: _____

Cause 2: *have poor study habits*   **Effect:** _____

Cause 3: _____   _____

Organization Pattern 2: One general cause results in several effects.

___ develop a bad attitude		___ lose energy
___ become ill due to stress		___ feel confused
___ Travelers have culture shock.		

Title: *Culture Shock*

Cause:_____

_____

Effect 1: _____

Effect 2: _____

Effect 3: _____

Effect 4: _____

Grammar: *For practice with* **Restrictive and Non-Restrictive Clauses,** *do Grammar Unit 10.*

Part 2: *Writing the first draft*

☞ Preparing to write the first draft

Strategy 1	Write advanced rather than simple ideas for a Cause and Effect Essay

Advanced ideas impress your reader. Often, they are unique; in other words, they are ideas that other students wouldn't think of.

Simple ideas are the type that lower-level students write.

Exercise 7

For Topic One and Topic Two below:

❶ Write **A** in the blank if the idea is **advanced.** (Four are advanced in Topic One and in Topic Two.)

❷ Write **S** in the blank if the idea is **simple.** (Two are simple in Topic One and in Topic Two.)

Topic One: *the reasons why people tell lies*

_A_ 1. They might actually not realize that it's a lie. They cannot face the truth, so they tell a lie.

____ 2. They want to hide the truth.

____ 3. They get pleasure in making people believe that something is true although it is really false.

____ 4. They need help. They can't admit that they have a problem, so they tell an obvious lie, but they secretly hope that someone will catch them and help them.

____ 5. They don't believe that the lie will hurt anyone, and actually, they sometimes even believe that the lie can improve a situation.

____ 6. They are bad people.

Topic Two: *the effects of students working at a part-time job*

____ 1. Students can earn extra money. (*a positive effec*t)

____ 2. Students can apply things that they learn in real-life situations to their classes. (*a positive effect*)

____ 3. Students might believe that their part-time job is so interesting that they quit school. Later, they might realize that the job isn't very challenging, and they will become bored. (*a negative effect*)

____4. Due to students' own experience at their part-time job, they appreciate the hard work that their parents (and others) are doing to support them, e.g. by paying for their tuition, so they are apt to study harder. (*a positive effect*)

____5. Students might not have enough time to focus on their assignments. (*a negative effect*)

____6. Students might not work seriously because they know their job is only part-time. After they graduate from school, and they apply for a full-time job, their former boss might give them a bad recommendation. (*a negative effect*)

Strategy 2   Consider several topics for your Cause and Effect Essay.

Exercise 8

❶ Choose *three* of the topics below.

❷ Decide the patterns that you could use:

• Several causes result in one general effect.
• One general cause results in several effects.

❸ Write a List of ideas for *all three topics. Try to write advanced ideas.* (See examples on p. 36).

❹ Next to each idea, write **A** if it is advanced and **S** if it is simple.

Topic Choices for a Cause and Effect Essay

____ What causes students to think that school is boring?

____ What causes parents to spoil their children? (or)
       What are the results of children who have been spoiled by their parents?

____ What causes some people to be afraid of getting married?

____ What causes teenagers to rebel against their parents?

____ What causes people to feel stress? (or) What are the effects of stress?

____ What are the causes of divorce? (or) What are the effects of divorce?

____ Think about a problem in your country. What are the causes of the problem? (or)
       What are the effects that the problem has had on your country or on you?

____ What causes a video game to be popular?

____ What are the causes of drug or alcohol abuse? (or)
       What are the effects of drug or alcohol abuse?

____ What causes people to believe in superstitions? (or)
       What are the effects that superstitions have on people?

____ What are the reasons for why I am living apart from my parents? (or)
       What are the effects that living apart from my parents has had on me?

____ Think about the methods that your parents (or others) used when raising you.
       What are the effects that those methods had on you?

____ other topic (*Tell your teacher before writing.*)

Pattern 1: (Several causes; one effect)

Topic: *Smoking*

Effect: Some people like to smoke cigarettes. There are several reasons why they smoke.

Cause 1: Some young people think smoking makes them seem more mature.
Cause 2: Smoking helps some people feel relieved of stress.
Cause 3: It gives people something to do with their hands.
Cause 4: Some people are entertained by blowing smoke out of their mouths.

Pattern 2: (One cause; several effects)

Topic: *Moving often*

Cause: Because of parents' jobs, some families must move often to new cities. Moving often can have both positive and negative effects on the children.

Effect 1: Children are unable to develop close relationships with friends. *(negative effect)*
Effect 2: Children lose a sense of stability. *(negative effect)*
Effect 3: Children develop independence and self-confidence. *(positive effect)*
Effect 4: Children develop closer relationships with siblings. *(positive effect)*

☞ First draft assignment — Write the first draft

Exercise 9: Write a first draft of a *Cause and Effect Essay.*

❶ Choose one of the topics from Exercise 8 on page 37.
❷ Write a first draft with the main ideas and a few details. *(See page 34 for sample first drafts.)*

Grammar: *For practice with* **Transitional Expressions and Conjunctions,** *do Grammar Unit 11.*

Part 3: *Writing the second draft*

☛ Preparing to write the second draft

(Think about improving your first draft while you do these exercises:
◆ *Adding details, p. 39;* ◆ *Writing advanced thesis statements, p. 43;* ◆ *Summing up the point, p. 46;*
◆ *Avoiding overgeneralizations, p. 48;* ◆ *7 types of introduction, p. 50;* ◆ *5 types of conclusion, p. 53;*
◆ *Using hypothetical situations in explanations, p. 57;* ◆ *Applying strategies, p. 58)*

Strategy 3	Add details to make your ideas clearer and more interesting.

Exercise 10

❶ Read the first drafts. Note the Δ symbol. Details will be added here.
❷ In the second drafts, details have been added. Fill in the blanks with words from the boxes.

Words for paragraphs 1 and 2

____ van   ____ lion   ____ say   ____ killed   ____ prepared   ____ nightmares

---

1. (**First draft**): Parents need to be aware of the types of TV programs that their children watch. Some shows contain scenes that may upset children. Δ Other programs may not be appropriate subjects for them.

(**Second draft** *with details added in italics where Δ appears*): Parents need to be aware of the types of TV programs that their children watch. Some shows contain scenes that may upset children. Δ Horror movies, for example, can cause children to have _____ _____. Also, scenes of animals being _____ – for example, a _____ ____ killing a deer – can be traumatic. Other programs may not be appropriate subjects for them.

2. (**First draft**): In a nursing home, elderly people have all the comforts that they need. Δ Also, they have other people to talk to.

(**Second draft** *with added details*): In a nursing home, elderly people have all the comforts that they need. Δ Let's _____ that a man who had been married for 60 years suddenly loses his wife. He may not be interested in cooking, doing the laundry, or cleaning his house. However, if he moves into a nursing home, all of his meals will be _____ __ for him, and someone will clean his room. If he wants to go shopping, nursing homes usually have a _____ that can take residents on shopping trips. Also, he will have other people to talk to.

Words for paragraphs 3 and 4					
___ talk	___ instance	___ relaxation	___ alone	___ energetic	___ complete

3. (**First draft**): Some people don't realize that, to have an enjoyable camping trip, we need to plan carefully in advance. First, we should decide whom to go with. Δ

(**Second draft** *with added details*): Some people don't realize that to have an enjoyable camping trip, we need to plan carefully in advance. First, we should decide whom to go with. Δ If our purpose is to get a lot of exercise, we should choose an _____ partner. If we just want to have fun, it would be good to include someone who likes to _____. However, if we want some quiet time to think, we may choose to go _____.

4. (**First draft**): In order to be successful in college, students need to manage their daily routine wisely Δ and develop good study habits.

(**Second draft** *with added details*): In order to be successful in college, students need to manage their daily routine wisely . Δ For _____, they should go to bed at the same time every night in order to get enough sleep. They need to get up early enough to eat a _____ breakfast before leaving for class. In addition, they need to schedule some time every day for _____ and exercise. They also need to develop good study habits.

Exercise 11

Add details to the first draft where this symbol "Δ" appears. (Write on other paper.)

1 . (**First draft**): If foreigners want to move to my country, they should know some important aspects about it. First, my country is <u>more expensive / less expensive</u> than many other countries. Δ This might affect foreigners' plans. ^(Choose.)

(**Second draft**: *Add details at the "Δ" symbol.*):

2. (**First draft**): When we are shopping for a new _____, we should consider
^(Fill in the blank.)
certain <u>features / factors</u>. Δ Also, we need to consider the price.
^(Choose.)

(**Second draft**: Add details at the "Δ" symbol.):

3. (**First draft**): For my sister, last year was not a good year. First, she had some health problems. Δ Second, she lost her job. Δ

(**Second draft**: Add details at the "Δ" symbols.):

Exercise 12

❶ Add a "Δ" where you can add details to the paragraphs.

❷ Add details in places where you put the "Δ" symbol.

1. (**First draft**): There are several reasons why I'm planning to look for a new roommate. My present roommate and I are completely different from each other. He/ She wears strange
clothes. Also, he/she has some unusual habits.   _(Choose.)
  _(Choose.)

(**Second draft**: Add details at the "Δ" symbol(s).):

2. (**First draft**): I once traveled to _____. I was
  _(Fill in the blank)
impressed with certain aspects of that place. However, I didn't like some others.

(**Second draft**: Add details at the "Δ" symbol(s).):

3. (**First draft**): People in my parents' generation and mine are different in a number of ways. One important difference concerns technology. In addition, my parents' generation seems concerned about the dating habits of my generation.

(**Second draft**: Add details at the "Δ" symbol(s).):

Strategy 4   Write an advanced-style thesis statement.

Exercise 13

Fill in the blanks with the thesis statements from the box.

Thesis Statement Choices

___ In this essay, I will describe an important childhood experience that I had and explain how it changed my life.

___ There are three types of teachers in our school: funny, serious, and odd.

___ In this essay, I will explain the procedure which a trainer should follow in order to teach a horse how to jump.

___ My brother is good at meeting new people.

___ Most people want a good marriage.

___ An unborn child (fetus) can suffer serious effects if its mother drinks alcohol while pregnant.

Topic 1: *teachers*

____***Weak* Thesis Statement**: There are many teachers in our school.
   Working Thesis Statement *(better)*: In this essay, I will describe the three types of teachers in our school: funny, serious, and odd.
   Advanced-style Thesis Statement *(best)*: _____

   _____

Topic 2: *marriage*

____***Weak* Thesis**: _____
   Working Thesis *(better)*: This essay will focus on the four important characteristics in a good marriage.
   Advanced-style Thesis *(best)*: A good marriage should have four important characteristics.

Topic 3: *a meaningful experience*

____***Weak* Thesis**: I once had a meaningful experience.
   Working Thesis *(better)*: _____

   _____

   Advanced-style Thesis *(best)*: My life was greatly changed by an experience that I had as a child.

Topic 4: *alcohol*

_____*Weak* **Thesis**: Alcohol can cause problems.

Working Thesis *(better)*: The purpose of this paper is to explain the dangerous effects that alcohol can have on a fetus when pregnant women drink.

Advanced-style Thesis *(best)*: _____

_____

Topic 5: *meeting people*

_____*Weak* **Thesis**: _____

Working Thesis *(better)*: This essay will describe the techniques that my brother uses to meet new people.

Advanced-style Thesis *(best)*: Meeting new people is a challenge for many individuals, but by using my brother's techniques, even shy people will be able to be successful at it.

Topic 6: *training a horse*

_____*Weak* **Thesis**: Training a horse takes a lot of time.

Working Thesis *(better)*: _____

_____

Advanced-style Thesis *(best)*: In order to teach a horse how to jump, a trainer should follow this procedure.

Exercise 14

Fill in the blanks with various forms of the thesis statements.

Topic 1: *returning home after living abroad*

_____*Weak* **Thesis Statement**: Returning home after living abroad is a strange feeling.

Working Thesis Statement *(better)*: This essay will focus on the most common emotions that students feel when they return home after living in a foreign country.

Advanced-style Thesis Statement *(best)*: _____

_____

Topic 2: *famous people*

____*Weak* **Thesis**: President Abraham Lincoln was a famous person, but he was sometimes depressed.
    Working Thesis *(better)*: _____
    _____

    Advanced-style Thesis *(best)*: Many people who have heard of Lincoln do not know about his struggles with depression.

Topic 3: *part-time jobs*

____*Weak* **Thesis**: _____
    Working Thesis *(better)*: The purpose of this essay is to convince the reader that high school students should not have part-time jobs.
    Advanced-style Thesis *(best)*: High school students should not have part-time jobs because of the negative effects these jobs can have on the students.

Exercise 15

❶ Choose three of the topics below.
❷ Write a **Weak Thesis Statement.**
❸ Write a **Working Thesis Statement**.
❹ Write an **Advanced-style Thesis Statement.**

Choice of Topics

___ life on other planets	___ food	___ cars	___ art	___ music
___ making spaghetti	___ love	___ a problem	___ war	___ crime
___ shoes	___ travel	___ a book	___ disease	
___ (other: You decide on a topic.)				

Use This Format

Topic: _____

Weak Thesis Statement: _____

Working Thesis Statement *(better)*: _____

Advanced-style Thesis *(best)*: _____

_____

Grammar: *For a review of* **Transirional Exprssions, Conjunctions, Clauses, and Reduced Clauses**, *do Grammar Unit 12.*

Strategy 5   Make your ideas clearer with summary statements.

Expressions for Summarizing

- To summarize,
- In other words,

- In sum,
- In summary,

- To sum up,
- In short,

Exercise 16: Fill in the blanks with the sentences in the box.

_____ **To sum up**, more and more women have become politically active.

_____ **In other words,** if people thought something looked worthless, they tended to throw it in the garbage rather than try to recycle it.

---

1. Researchers have found that people will put whole pieces of paper in a recycling bin, but if the paper was torn in pieces, they would throw them in a garbage bin. Similarly, if a can was dented or smashed, they would throw that in the garbage, but if it was intact (not smashed), they would place it in a recycling bin. _____

   _____

2. Several years ago, there were no women in the important government positions in my state. Today, the mayor of my city, the governor, and one of the senators are all women. _____

   _____

   _____

   _____

Exercise 17

❶ Choose one of the "expressions for summarizing."

❷ Write a one-sentence summary in order to finish the paragraphs.

1. People who live in Wisconsin enjoy cross-country skiing during the long winter months. Fishing attracts many people starting in the spring. During the summer, doing water sports at Wisconsin's many lakes is also very popular. In addition, hiking, which is always enjoyable, is especially fun in the cool autumn. _____

   _____

2. Joe Ogdon has been a garbage collector for 20 years. Every day, he collects garbage from about 750 homes. He doesn't especially like garbage, and he often has to listen to people making jokes about his job. However, he enjoys working outside, and he likes to work alone. Also, he gets four weeks' vacation a year, has a great retirement plan, and has good health insurance. He gets paid a nice salary of $19 an hour, which is about $40,000 a year. _____

   _____

   _____

3. Recently, the number of teenage members in gangs in the U.S. has doubled. We also hear much about the problems of drug use, not only of marijuana but also of cocaine, among young people. Destruction of school property, assaults on teachers and truancy are just a few of the many problems in our schools. Every day, we read in the newspaper about young people using guns to settle disputes with others. _____

_____

4. A Greek person once commented that a Greek, any Greek, would die of loneliness immediately, if left alone on a remote, deserted island for more than 24 hours. Greeks spend, on the average, eight hours a day in conversation with fellow-Greeks. They can sit contentedly for hours and hours over a tiny cup of coffee discussing the events of the world with other people. _____

_____

_____

5. A recent survey of American teenagers found that 93% of them feel happy "most" or "some" of the time. Only 24% felt depressed. Over 76% agreed that "I am pretty confident that things will work out for me," while only 21% said "I'm not sure how things will work out for me."

_____

_____

Exercise 18

❶ Choose two of the topics below.
❷ Write a paragraph for each. Include an "expression for summarizing" and a summary statement.

Possible Topics

___ food	___ an animal	___ a hobby	___ a job
___ school	___ travel	___ foreign places	___ foreign people
___ technology	___ a family member	___ other	

Strategy 6   Make your style more advanced by avoiding overgeneralizations.

Exercise 19

❶ Look again at the two sample *Cause and Effect* Essays on page 34.

❷ Copy the style which is used to avoid over-generalizations.

❸ <u>Underline</u> the expressions.

Overgeneralizations	Avoiding overgeneralizations
a. (See page 34, paragraph 1.) However, students who are unprepared fail.	a. However, students who are unprepared <u>are likely to</u> fail.
b. (¶ 2) Students oversleep…	b.
c. (¶ 4) Finally, students fail …	c.
d. (¶ 4)… they perform poorly on assignments.	d.
e. (¶ 6) After arriving in a foreign country, people feel excited …	e.

Overgeneralizations	Avoiding overgeneralizations
f. (¶ 6) Travelers with culture shock experience a variety …	f.
g. (¶ 7) … the traveler has problems …	g.
h. (¶ 8) The traveler just wants to stay in bed …	h.
i. (¶ 9) …travelers with culture shock become ill …	i.
j. (¶ 9) … for them to catch a cold or …	j. I_____ i_____ n_____ u_____ f_____ ….
k. (¶ 10) … because experiences do not meet the traveler's expectations, they blame the people or culture …	k.
l. (¶ 11) … they can overcome these uncomfortable feelings.	l.

Strategy 7   Write an interesting introduction. Choose from seven types.

Seven Introduction Techniques

1 Quotation
2 Surprising idea
3 Statistics (numbers)
4 Dramatic introduction

5 News
6 Tell your experience
7 Common knowledge

Exercise 20

For each introduction below, fill in the blanks with the thesis statements from the box.

Thesis Statements Choices
for the introductory paragraphs below

___ There are several reasons why a large number of college graduates are attracted to my town.

___ People, like me, who spend a lot of time at the computer should be aware that extensive use can cause physical problems.

___ Someone who is planning to shop for a car may want to consider the following factors before making a final choice.

___ In fact, there are several causes for the war in my country.

X ___ Today, unfortunately, other forms of discrimination can still be found.

___ In order to stay healthy, we should understand how people actually do catch colds and how colds can be prevented.

___ In fact, they are trying some unique ways to solve their problems in education.

---

1. **Quotation** *(You can use the words of a famous person, a friend, a relative, etc.)*

Example topic: *War in My Country*

My uncle often used to say, "Peace is worth fighting for." Although my uncle hated war, he felt that sometimes it was necessary. Of course, everyone in my country wants peace, but there has been fighting there recently. *In fact, there are several causes for*

the war in my country.

2. Surprising Idea

Example topic: *Getting Sick with a Cold*

Contrary to what many people believe, we do not catch colds because cold air blows on us. Also, we don't catch a cold because we didn't wear a hat on a cold day, or because someone with a cold sneezed or coughed on us. _____

_____

_____

3. Statistics *(numbers)*

Example topic: *Education Level of Residents in My Hometown*

In my hometown, Eastwood, 63% of the citizens are college graduates. In the neighboring town, Westmont, only 11% have college degrees. _____

_____

_____

4. Dramatic Introduction *(a brief story)*

Example topic: **Racial Discrimination Today**

The bus door opened. The passengers climbed into the air-conditioned bus, happy to escape the terrible heat. One last person got on the bus carrying a heavy load of packages. She was old, and she was black. She sat in the first seat that she could find, which was near the driver. "You can't sit there," the driver said. "All blacks must sit in the back!"

This kind of discrimination was common 50 years ago but nowadays is prohibited by law. _____

_____

_____

5. News *(from the newspaper, magazine, or TV report)*

Example topic: *Solving Problems in Schools*

In *Newstime* magazine, it was recently reported that many bigger cities in the U.S., e.g. Chicago and New York, are having problems finding teachers because of the violence that occurs in their schools every day. Students with family, drug, and alcohol problems make life difficult for teachers. Seattle, however, is determined to make its schools a good place to study. _____

_____

_____

6. Tell an Experience with the Topic

Example topic: *Computer Health Hazards*

Last May, I started feeling a sharp pain in my elbow. I couldn't imagine what the cause of the pain could be; I hadn't bumped it or lifted anything heavy. One day, after I'd been working at my computer for three hours straight, it became worse than ever before. That led me to discover the cause of my injury: my computer keyboard. _____

_____

_____

7. Common Knowedge

Example topic: *Buying a car*

Many people would agree that a car is a necessity of modern life. Car companies produce flashy ads in order to convince us to buy their most expensive models. However, a high-priced or sporty-looking car may not be the one that fits our lifestyle the best.

_____

_____

Exercise 21

❶ Choose <u>three of the topics</u> below.
❷ Write an ***introduction and thesis statement only*** for each. Try to use a different introduction type for each. <u>Underline the thesis statements</u>.
❸ Tell what introduction type you used for each.
(See page 50 for a list of seven types of introductions.)

Choice of Topics

___ sports	___ my best friend	___ poor sleeping habits
___ caring for the elderly	___ how to improve our English	___ global warming
___ dating	___ job interviews	___ (You choose a topic.)
___ culture shock	___ changing fashions	
___ taking care of children	___ if I were rich	
___ a great book/movie	___ social media	

Use This Format

1. Topic: *politics*

   Introduction Type: *Dramatic Introduction*

   Introduction & Thesis statement: _____ ...

Strategy 8   Write an interesting conclusion:

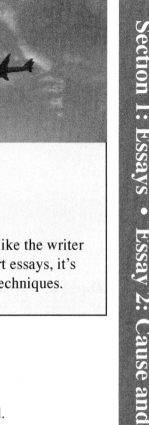

Five Conclusion Techniques

1 Quotation
2 Complete the dramatic introduction
3 Complete the experience with the topic from the introduction
4 Explain why the information in the essay is important
5 Summarize the thesis statement and main points of the essay*

*In short essays of 2 or 3 pages, the summary conclusion can sound like the writer is just repeating information which the reader had just read. For short essays, it's often more interesting if the writer uses one of the other conclusion techniques.

Exercise 22

❶ Read the sample introductions, outlines of the body, and conclusions below.
❷ After each conclusion, write the type of "Conclusion Technique" that is used.
❸ Use each conclusion type <u>one time</u>.

Topic 1: *Fear of flying*

Introduction

We often hear that airplane travel is much safer than traveling by car. Nevertheless, many people feel insecure as plane passengers. Their stress level is often especially raised during the landing. Although most passengers hope for smooth landings, they should know that "smoothies" are not always safer than "hard" landings.

Outline of the body

a. Hard landings are better under certain weather conditions (e.g. rain).
b. To make smooth landings, pilots need a lot of runway space.

Conclusion

It's important for passengers to realize that bumps during landings are natural. They should also understand that a hard landing does not mean the plane is about to crash, but rather, it means that the pilot is probably using the safest type of landing for those conditions. With this knowledge, passengers should be able to relax more when their plane is landing.

Conclusion Technique: _____

Topic 2: *Effects of the media on society*

Introduction

Early one Sunday, Jerry Lokey was driving his car on his way to a friend's house when he saw something strange. A three-year-old boy was walking alone and dangerously close to the busy highway. Jerry stopped his car in the road next to the boy but was not sure what he should do. If Jerry let the boy continue walking along the road, he might be hit by a speeding car. However, if he put the boy in his car, someone might see him and accuse him of kidnapping. As Jerry slowed down and wondered what to do, other drivers sped past him shouting, "Get out of the way!" and honked their horns.

We often hear complaints from the older generation about people nowadays not helping others as much as they did years ago. The older generation tends to blame this trend on a weak moral character among younger people. However, it seems that it is not a result of a change in morals, but rather a result of the media's obsession with negative stories that has caused people to hesitate to help others.

Outline of the body

a. Newspapers use horrible crime stories to sell more copies.
b. The media rarely tells stories about people helping other people.
c. TV news programs try to include "good" stories but they tend to show them near the end of the program.

Conclusion

Jerry Lokey never left his car. Instead, he kept driving slowly next to the boy, ignoring the honks of other drivers. Finally, he was able to call out for help to a woman in another car. She used her cell phone to call the police, who came to rescue the boy. Like Jerry, she too was afraid to pick up the boy. It is unfortunate, but because of the desire by TV news programs to get higher ratings and the need by newspapers and magazines to sell more copies, shocking stories are making people afraid to help others in need.

Conclusion Technique: _____

Topic 3: *Advantages and disadvantages of email*

Introduction

Email has become a vital part of both business and personal communication. People think of it as something that appears and disappears in an on-screen mailbox at the click of a mouse. Unfortunately, anyone who does not realize that email also has risks could face serious problems. Although email has some positive points, there is also possible danger.

Outline of the body

a. Positive: cheap, easy, and time-efficient way to stay in touch with others
b. Negative: easy to mistakenly click the "send" button and send an embarrassing message to the wrong person

Conclusion

All email users should realize that even though email is an enjoyable way to communicate, it also can unexpectedly cause the end of friendships. My teacher once said, "It's a good idea to ask yourself honestly if email is the best way to send a certain message."

Conclusion Technique: _____

Topic 4: *Intercultural communication*

Introduction

As more companies become multinational, and as more American employees travel abroad to do business, there is a need to know how to deal with other cultures. These Americans will have to be especially careful about the topics they discuss, how they express their opinions, and when it is proper to talk about business.

Outline of the body

a. Unlike in American culture, in some other cultures it is acceptable to discuss politics and religion.
b. Americans should avoid expressing negative feelings about a colleague's country.
c. In social situations, Americans should not discuss business unless others mention it first.
d. People in some other countries think that it is more important to know who you are than what your past experience is.

Conclusion

In conclusion, American business travelers abroad need to be sensitive to other cultures. They should be aware that certain topics like politics and religion might be discussed. Also, they need to be careful when expressing feelings about a foreign culture. They ought to be ready to let others take the lead in conversations. And finally, they must be aware that, in certain situations, it may not be a good idea to talk about work.

Conclusion Technique: _____

Topic 5: *A problem*

Introduction

I have a gambling problem. A year ago, if someone had told me I was a gambling addict, I would have laughed at them. I thought that I just enjoyed gambling like many other people. I have discovered, though, that gambling was having a negative effect on my life. I also learned that there are ways to find out if someone is a compulsive gambler.

Outline of the body

a. Does gambling make the home life unhappy?
b. After winning, does the gambler have a strong desire to continue and win more?
c. Does the gambler gamble in order to escape problems?
d. Does gambling interfere with sleep?

Conclusion

After analyzing the effects that gambling was having on my home life, I realized that I had a serious problem. Once I acknowledged this, I was able to seek help from a professional therapist. Over the past few months, I have learned how to control the desire to gamble, and feel I am now on the road to recovery.

Conclusion Technique: _____

Grammar: *For a review of* **Commas** *and* **Semicolons**, *do Grammar Unit 13.*

Strategy 9

Make your ideas clearer with hypothetical situations.

(A hypothetical situation is one that you imagine or make up.)

Note: *It is acceptable to use "you" in a hypothetical situation.*

Expressions for Introducing a Hypothetical Situation

- Let's say that . . .
- Imagine that . . .
- For example, if . . .

Exercise 23: Fill in the blanks with the words from the box.

____ Imagine that a 16-year-old boy named Jim
____ Let's say that you always dreamed of visiting Hawaii.
____ For example, if a man has three drinks in an hour, it
____ begin throwing rocks, too.
____ his brain too much time
____ as nice as the ones in the movies

Topic 1: *Causes of Culture Shock*

The fourth effect is the development of a bad attitude toward the new culture. In some cases, because experiences do not meet the traveler's expectations, they are likely to blame the people for not being open. _____
As a child, you often saw movies that took place in Hawaii, and everyone looked as if they were having fun staying in gorgeous hotels, walking on the beach, and surfing. Finally, you take a trip there, but soon after you arrive, you find that your hotel isn't _____, the beaches are crowded, and surfing is scary.

Topic 2: *Causes of Riots*

In addition to anger, another reason why people riot is simply because other people around them are doing it. _____ goes to a championship football game with five of his teenage friends. Jim comes from a good family and has never been in trouble. His team wins the championship, and he leaves the stadium with thousands of other happy fans. The nervous excitement causes somebody to throw a rock , which breaks a window in a store. Everyone cheers. Then, others throw rocks, and someone starts a fire. Soon Jim and his friends _____
_____

Topic 3: *The Results of Driving after Drinking*

A third effect that a driver will feel while driving after drinking is an inability to stop the car quickly. _____ will cause his reflexes to slow down. If he starts to drive and suddenly sees a child run out into the street in front of him, he will not be able to stop in time because it will take _____ _____ to tell his foot to step on the brake.

Exercise 24

❶ Choose <u>two of the topics</u> below and write paragraphs like those in Exercise 23.
❷ Write a one-sentence "introduction" (i.e., topic sentence) to the paragraph.
❸ Somewhere in the paragraph, describe a hypothetical situation.

Paragraph Topics

Explain . . .

• *how an older person can look younger*

• *how to convince a policeman not to give us a ticket*

• *how to make new friends at school*

• *the effects that social media have on young people*

• *what causes a family to have close relationships*

• *what causes video games to be so popular*

• *which is better: living alone or with a roommate*

• *whether high school students should wear uniforms*

Strategy 10   Apply the strategies and improve your style.

Exercise 25

❶ The second draft of the essay "Failing in College" *(on page 59)* includes details added to the first draft on page 34. To impove this draft, choose the words and phrases given in the box and write them in the blanks. This sample essay is probably shorter than the one that you will write for your final draft.
❷ At the end of the paragraph, write the introduction type *(on page 50)*, the strategy, or the conclusion type *(on page 53)*. **Hint:** for strategies, use *example, summing up,* or *hypothetical situation.*

Paragraphs 1-2:
___ decisions (such as when to go to bed, when to get up, or when to study)
_X_ which means that it is the first time for them to make daily decisions
___ sacrifice recreational activities for studying

Paragraph 3:
___ In addition to weak self-discipline
___ failure, students need to develop good ones.
___ Because high school courses are quite different

Paragraphs 4-5:
___ However, in the end, it is
___ In sum, students need strong basic skills
___ it's important for students to know that

Failing in College

¹ According to a recent news article, 30% of freshman students our college do not return after their first semester. For many freshmen, it is the first time for them to be away from home, *which means that it is the first time for them to make daily decisions* about how they should spend their time. For other freshmen, the problem is that high school did not prepare them well. In fact, freshman students drop out of college for reasons that are often connected to inexperience or poor preparation. *Introduction Type:* _____

² The first cause of students failing in college is their lack of self-discipline. Imagine that a student named Tom just left home for the first time. Before he entered college, many important _____ were made by his parents. As a result, Tom now often has problems forcing himself to get up in time for classes or to_____ _____
_____. *Strategy:* _____

³ _____ , another reason why students fail in college is poor study habits. _____ from college courses, many college freshmen must develop new systems for studying. For example, they need to know how to take accurate notes during lecture classes and also how to use those notes to prepare for tests and to write reports. Because study habits can make the difference between success and _____ *Strategy:* _____

⁴ A third reason why students fail is because of their weak basic skills. It is not unusual for students to have sufficient knowledge in academic subjects, such as science, but to be weak in certain skills, such as writing. _____.
Strategy: _____

⁵ In conclusion, _____ to be successful in college, they will need to be more responsible than they were in high school. Parents and high school teachers can help students develop the self-discipline, proper study habits, and basic skills that they will need to be successful. _____ the students themselves who must take responsibility. *Conclusion Type:*_____

Exercise 26

Fill in the "List of Main Ideas" below about the essay above, "Failing in College."

Failing in College
List of main ideas

Working thesis: This paper will focus on the reasons why some students fail in college.

1. First cause: lack of **self- d**_____
   a. Parents made decisions.
   b. Problems getting up and sacrificing **r**_____ **a**_____

2. Second cause: poor **s**_____ **h**_____
   a. Need to know how to **t**_____ **n**_____

3. Third cause: weak **b**_____ **s**_____

☞ Second draft assignment — Write the second draft

Exercise 27: Write a second draft of the *Cause and Effect Essay* that you wrote on page 38.

❶ Write a working thesis statement and list of main ideas for the first draft of your essay.

❷ Write a second draft of your Cause and Effect Essay. Try to improve your first draft by using these strategies:

Make your ideas clearer and more interesting by:

____ adding details and examples. *(See page 39.)*

____ summing up the main point of a paragraph. *(See page 46.)*

____ using hypothetical situations. *(See page 57.)*

Make your thesis statement sound more advanced. *(See page 43.)*

Make your style sound more advanced by avoiding overgeneralizations. *(See page 48.)*

Write an interesting introduction. *(See page 50.)*

Write an interesting conclusion. *(See page 53.)*

Grammar: *For practice with* **Gerunds and Participles,** *do Grammar Unit 14.*

Fluency Writing: **While working on your second draft, do a Fluency Writing. After finishing the Fluency Writing, continue working on your second draft.**

Part 4: *Writing the final draft*

☛ Preparing to write the final draft, using peer-editing

Strategy 11 Listen to a partner read your essay to you.

Exercise 28

After you finish your second draft:

❶ Exchange essays with a classmate.
❷ Read your classmate's essay silently.
❸ Read your classmate's essay aloud to them.
❹ Your classmate will read your essay aloud to you.
    You can ask them to stop reading at any time
    and ask "peer-editing"-type questions.

(You do not have to make any changes to your essay if you do not want to.)

☛ Final draft assignment — Write the final draft

Exercise 29

Write a final draft of the *Cause and Effect Essay* that you began on page 38.

Grammar: *For practice with* **Infinitives**, *do Grammar Unit 15.*

To the teacher: see the *Teacher's Manual* for these photocopyable materials:

• **Cause and Effect Check-list**
• **Cause and Effect Evaluation Form**
• **Cause and Effect In-class Essay Topics**

Essay 3: Extended Definition

(An extended definition essay describes a word or concept in detail.)

Fluency Writing: Before starting this unit, do a Fluency Writing from Section 2. After finishing, begin working individually on the following exercises.

Part 1: *Focusing on the unique features*

There are five strategies that may be used to extend a definition. Examples are given below.

Definition Strategy	Word	Example of the Strategy
1. **Give an example**	*success*	Bill Gates is someone who has had success. He had the natural ability and motivation to accomplish his goals of developing software.
2. **Explain the parts** *(characteristics, aspects, conditions, requirements)*	*pity*	There are three conditions necessary before we can express pity. One is that we must notice someone in an unfortunate situation. Also, we must feel that that person was a victim, in other words, not responsible for their bad luck. And third, we need to feel that, if possible, we would like to improve that person's situation.
3. **Use similar terms to compare and contrast**	*rival*	The word "rival" has a lot in common with "enemy." We are competing with both; they both motivate us to perform better. However, there are some differences between them. We may actually like our rival. In fact, a rival may be our best friend. On the other hand, we don't feel affection for our enemy.
4. **Use negation** *(what the word does **not** mean)* [e.g. ___(word)___ *does not necessarily mean what most people think it does.]*	Example 1 *good leader* Example 2 *successful*	A good leader is *not* someone who *just* tells others what to do. Instead, a good leader inspires others to do good work. Being successful *does not necessarily* mean winning. A person can lose a game, for example, but still be successful in earning the respect of their teammates by trying hard.
5. **Tell the history** *(either its origin or your first experience with the word)* (**History of the word** does **not** mean to tell a **story** with the word.) (You can use a dictionary to find the origin.)	*awesome*	Several years ago, "awesome" was used to describe something that was truly outstanding or spectacular. If something was awesome, it was almost one-of-a-kind. For example, the Great Wall of China was awesome. Recently, though, people use it to describe almost anything. For instance, people will use it to describe a good movie, their dog, or even their favorite ice cream.

Strategy 1   Give an example.

A good example helps the reader understand the word more clearly.

____ (**weak example**) "anger":

Anger is not an attractive characteristic. For example, my brother often feels anger. *(This is weak because the reader might think anger means "depressed" or "confused.")*

____ (**good example**) "anger":

(If you use an example of a person, tell the name of that person or make up a name.) Anger is not an attractive characteristic. For example, my brother, Tim, often feels anger; if he gets upset, his face turns red, and he yells.

Exercise 1

❶ Write **Good** if the paragraph gives an example that helps the reader understand the word more clearly.

❷ Write **Weak** if the paragraph does not give an example that helps the reader understand the word.

_____ 1. "beautiful": There are many beautiful places in the U.S. For example, Hawaii is a beautiful place.

_____ 2. "beautiful": An example of a beautiful place is Hawaii. It has white sand between the blue ocean and green forests. It also has colorful sunsets.

_____ 3. "strange": My roommate, Jamie, is someone whom I consider to be strange. Because of his frustrating habits, I don't like to go to parties with him.

_____ 4. "strange": My roommate, Jamie, is someone whom I consider to be strange. He sometimes talks to himself and stares at other people. As a result, I don't like to go to parties with him.

Strategy 2   Explain the parts (characteristics, aspects, conditions, requirements).

Exercise 2: Fill in the blanks with the words from the box.

___ three requirements   ___ opinions   ___ listener   ___ help

✗ aspects   ___ characteristics   ___ vote   ___ expression

___ laugh

1. a fair election   A fair election has several important _____*aspects*_____. First, all candidates must have an equal chance to explain their _____. Second, every voter can have only one vote. In addition, no voter should be afraid to _____ for whomever they want.

2. buddies   For friends to be considered buddies, there are _____. To start with, buddies are people whom you want to spend all your time with. Also, they make you feel happy, and you probably _____ a lot when you are together. Finally, they are ready to _____ you at any time even if you don't ask.

3. a *destle* *   "Destle"* is a word in my language used to describe a type of person. A *destle* has some interesting _____. It is always an older man who never shows any emotions. Even if something wonderful or terrible happens to him, the _____ on his face never changes. Also, a *destle* doesn't like to talk much. And on top of that, he is a good _____. As a result, people like to ask for his advice on a variety of topics.

* *destle* is an imaginary word.

Strategy 3   Use similar terms to compare and contrast.

To compare and contrast, the writer should explain how the two words are both similar and different.

Exercise 3

❶ Write **Both** if the definition includes both similarities and differences
❷ Write **Not Complete** if it includes only one of them.

_____ 1. "rebel" (noun): When we use the word "rebel," we often imagine a "revolutionary." Both words refer to people who disagree with the leadership of an organization, company, or government.

_____ 2. "rebel" (noun): When we use the word "rebel," we often imagine a "revolutionary." Both words refer to people who disagree with the leadership of an organization, company, or government. However, unlike a revolutionary, who will try to completely change how an organization, company, or government operates, a rebel will complain about a policy and try to change it.

_____ 3. "*frunge*"*: In my language, we use *frunge* to describe a surprising situation. Both "a surprise" and a *frunge* mean something unexpected happened. On the other hand, there is a difference between them. Usually, the emotion from a surprise soon ends, but not from a *frunge*. For example, we would describe the sudden death of a close friend in a car accident as a *frunge* because the shock and sadness we feel will continue for months and even years after the event.

* *frung* is an imaginary word.

_____ 4. "desire" (verb): If we desire something, it means we want it. For example, I may desire to have a large house with a swimming pool, which means the same as wanting those things.

Essay: *Extended Definition* • **Part 1:** *Focusing on the unique features* • **65**

Strategy 4   Use negation to define a word.

Negation tells what a word *does not* (only or necessarily) *mean*. Often, it is just a <u>unique</u> way to think about a word.

Common Phrases for Negation

_____ does not necessarily mean _____
(word)   (fill in)
     (Example: <u>Quiet</u> does not necessarily mean <u>shy</u>.)

_____ does not only mean _____
(word)   (fill in)
     (Example: <u>Beautiful</u> does not only mean <u>physical attractiveness</u>.)

_____ is not someone who just _____
(word)
     (Example: An <u>extrovert</u> is not someone who just <u>talks a lot</u>.)

_____ is not something that just _____
(word)
     (Example: A <u>good job</u> is not something that just <u>pays a lot of money</u>.)

Weak negation: *<u>Beautiful</u> does not mean <u>ugly</u>.* (This is obvious.)

Exercise 4

❶ Fill in the blanks with the words from the box.
❷ Double-underline the "Common Phrases for Negation" that were used.

___ evil	___ lose	_X_ problems	___ over and over
___ money	___ physical suffering	___ look good	

1. In contrast to what many people think, "happiness" <u><u>does not necessarily mean</u></u> that a person is free of _*problems*_____ . A person can have problems, yet still be happy if they have a positive attitude.

2. "Pain" does not only mean _____. It can also be mental.

3. Many people don't appreciate good shoes. Good shoes are not something that just _____. They are like our best friends because they are with us many hours every day.

4. There is a common misunderstanding about the word "diet." A diet does not necessarily mean a routine that we follow in order to _____ weight. My brother was on a diet to *gain* weight when he joined the football team.

5. A wealthy person is not someone who just has a lot of _____ . People who are truly wealthy feel as if they have everything that they want.

6. A bad leader is not someone who is just _____. A bad leader might be a good person who has weak leadership skills.

7. "A habit" does not necessarily mean something that we do _____. For example, we eat dinner every evening, but that doesn't mean that it is a habit.

Strategy 5   Tell the history.

- The history of a word means the origin of the word *or* your first experience with the word.
- To tell the history of a word does not mean to tell a story with the word in it.

Exercise 5

❶ Write **History** for the *four paragraphs* that tell a history of the word.
❷ Write **Not History** for the two paragraphs that do not tell a history of the word.

_____ 1. *buzz:* The first time I saw the word "buzz" I was in 3rd grade. It was in a story that we were reading. I asked my teacher what it meant. She didn't say anything but, instead, took all of us outside to the school garden. Because it was springtime, there were many bees in the garden. She told us to listen to the bees. "That sound is a buzz," she said.

_____ 2. *trust*: Jay was a very talented musician and computer specialist. After college, a famous band invited him to join them on tour. At the same time, a new software company offered him a job. Because he couldn't decide what to do, he asked his grandfather for advice. He told Jay to trust his inner voice.

_____ 3. *RSVP:* Often, invitations to a party or wedding will have the letters RSVP on them. This means that we should contact the sender to say whether or not we will be able to attend. The origin of RSVP is the French phrase, "*Repondez, s'il vous plait,*" which can be translated as "Respond, please."

_____ 4. *crazy:* The word "crazy" was first used to describe a person who was insane, in other words, a person with serious mental problems. Today, it is often used to describe a feeling of great enthusiasm. For example, we can say, "She is crazy about jazz." This means that she loves jazz music very much. It does not mean that she has a mental problem.

_____ 5. *mystery:* My dog, Duke, was my best friend for 15 years. Unfortunately, he died one day. Two days later, I heard something crying at my front door. When I looked out, I saw a puppy that looked just like Duke sitting there. Where this puppy came from is a mystery. In other words, nobody in my family and none of my neighbors or friends know how it got there.

_____ 6. *wai-shatsu:* In Japanese, we have the word "*wai-shatsu.*" It comes from the English word "white shirt." We began to use this word when Western-style business suits started to become common in Japan.

Essay: *Extended Definition* • **Part 1:** *Focusing on the unique features* • 67

Strategies for Defining a Word

___ Give an example   ___ Explain the parts   ___ Tell the history
___ Use similar terms to compare and contrast   ___ Use negation

Exercise 6: From the box above, identify the strategy used for each of these paragraphs.

Strategy	Word	Example of the Strategy
1. _____	*weird*	The word "weird" is similar in some ways to "strange." People who are strange and weird act in ways that are different from the average person. On the other hand, the words have different meanings. It seems that a weird person is apt to be a nonconformist; in other words, a weird person is intentionally different from the average person, but a strange person is different by nature.
2. _____	*foolish*	A foolish person is capable of making good decisions, but, for some reason, fails to do so.
3. _____	*bad* (slang)	I am sure that, like most people, I learned the word my 1970's, I heard "bad" used to mean "good" for the first time. On the radio, a man who was talking about his favorite basketball player said, "He is really bad!" Later, he said, "He has some bad moves!" In the context, I knew that he was using "bad" to mean "good."
4. _____	*leftovers*	There are two requirements in order for food to become leftovers. First, the person preparing the meal has to make more food than everyone can finish during the meal. Second, the food that is not eaten must be saved. In other words, it cannot be thrown out. At this point, the food can be called leftovers.
5. _____	*prince*	My mother often described someone as being a prince. For example, after my Uncle Jim fixed her car for free, she said, "Jim really is a prince." When my neighbor, Mr. Smith, visited her in the hospital, she called him a prince.

Exercise 7

❶ Choose <u>five of the words or concepts</u> below.

❷ Define them by using a "Definition Strategy" *(introduced on page 62)*. Try to use a different strategy for each one.

Use This Format

Word or concept: _____

Strategy: _____

Definition: _____

Option One

Choose an English expression. Here are some examples:

__ good friend	__ jealousy	__ courage
__ beauty	__ generosity	__ common sense
__ a lie	__ a good / bad teacher	__ loneliness
__ politeness	__ a good / bad parent	__ a slang expression (that you know)
__ wealth	__ creativity	__ failure
__ respect	__ embarrassed/embarrassment	__ a good / bad marriage
__ pride	__ a good / bad date	__ ashamed / shame
__ femininity	__ a good / bad spouse	__ maturity
__ masculinity	__ laziness	__ a good / bad education
__ prejudice	__ non-conformist	__ Choose another English word.

Option Two

Choose a word from your language that is difficult to translate directly. Here are some examples:

__ *baraka* (Arabic)	__ *schadenfreude* (German)	__ *khe tee sawaa* (Punjabi)
__ *yiqi* (Chinese)	__ *durhaka* (Indonsian)	__ *razlubit* (Russian)
__ *gianxi* (Chinese)	__ *tatemae* (Japanese)	__ *criollada* (Spanish)
__ *janteloven* (Dutch)	__ *youp gi* (Korean)	__ *gig* (Thai)
__ *taarof* (Farsi)	__ *saudade* (Portugese)	__ *cu chuoi* (Vietnamese)
__ *déjà-vu* (French)	__ *sahabat* (Malaysian)	__ (Choose different word.)

Grammar: *For a review of* **Gerunds and Infinitives**, *do Grammar Unit 16.*

Essay: *Extended Definition* • **Part 1:** *Focusing on the unique features* • **69**

Part 2: *Writing the first draft*

☛ Preparing to write the first draft
Extended Definition Essay, Style I: Define a Common Word in English.

Exercise 8

❶ Read the essay titled "Intelligence" below.
❷ In the blanks on the left, write the "Definition Strategy" that is used for each paragraph.

Strategies for Defining a Word

___ Give an example   ___ Explain the parts   ___ Tell the history
___ Use similar terms to compare and contrast   ___ Use negation

---

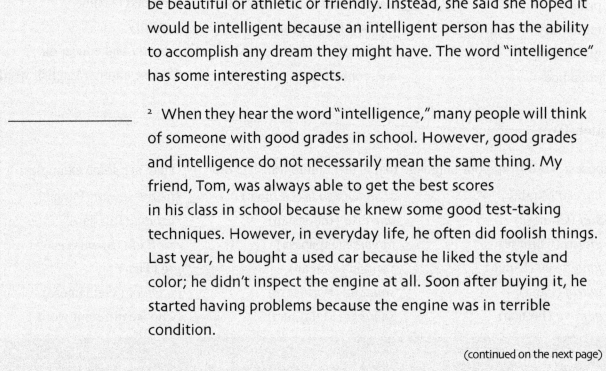

"Intelligence"

STRATEGY

INTRODUCTION
(no strategy used)

¹ My friend is expecting a baby soon. When I asked her what characteristics she hoped her baby would have, she gave an interesting answer. She did not say that she hoped that it would be beautiful or athletic or friendly. Instead, she said she hoped it would be intelligent because an intelligent person has the ability to accomplish any dream they might have. The word "intelligence" has some interesting aspects.

_____

² When they hear the word "intelligence," many people will think of someone with good grades in school. However, good grades and intelligence do not necessarily mean the same thing. My friend, Tom, was always able to get the best scores in his class in school because he knew some good test-taking techniques. However, in everyday life, he often did foolish things. Last year, he bought a used car because he liked the style and color; he didn't inspect the engine at all. Soon after buying it, he started having problems because the engine was in terrible condition.

(continued on the next page)

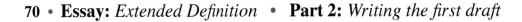

3   Intelligence is similar to cleverness in some ways, but it is different in other ways. A clever person, like an intelligent one, is better at some things than the average person. For example, my neighbor is very good at doing magic tricks. Unfortunately, he is not very good at doing much else. Therefore, he could be considered clever but not intelligent. An intelligent person can use their brain to do a large number of things well. A clever person is often limited to doing only a few things well.

4   There is a way that people can develop their intelligence. One important requirement is to focus. This means that, when learning something new, a person is giving total attention to it; in other words, they do not become distracted by anything else in the surroundings. The second requirement is to internalize. That is to say, the person really tries to remember the important aspects of the new knowledge. Another requirement is to apply. In other words, the person uses the information they are learning to accomplish a task or job.

5   An example of a person whom I consider to have intelligence is my brother. One day, a pipe broke in his house, but he had no experience with fixing such a problem. The first thing he did was to focus on a solution by referring to a book in the library and talking to a neighbor about how to repair pipes. After getting this information, he applied what he learned and was able to fix the problem.

CONCLUSION
(no strategy used)

6   It will be interesting to watch my friend's child grow. There is little doubt that she will provide the child with every opportunity to develop its intelligence. If the mother accomplishes her goal, the child can probably look forward to a very interesting life.

Extended Definition Essay, Style II: Define an English Word That is Difficult to Translate (directly) into Other Languages.

Exercise 9

Read the short, simple first draft of the essay titled "Is 'Fun' an English-only Concept?" Imagine that you have a classmate who wants your opinion about this first draft.

Is "Fun" an English-only Concept?

[1] The word "fun" seems to be difficult for speakers of other languages to translate accurately.

[2] "Fun" is such a common word in English that, as a student of French, I often wanted to use the French equivalent when communicating in French. French has the expression, "amusant," but the English equivalent, "amusing," does not quite match the meaning of "fun." When I think of "amusing" things, board games, card games, and puzzles come to mind. However, it seems that "fun" is not limited to just games.

[3] One aspect (or characteristic) of "fun" is that it almost always applies to enjoyable activities, rather than places that we enjoy. Another language that I know has the same word for "fun" and "cheerful." It is possible to say that a place is cheerful, such as in, "The child's bedroom is cheerful." However, we would not say, "The child's bedroom is fun."

[4] There is more to "fun" than the characteristics mentioned above; it is also an activity that has our complete attention. The following episode introduces another important aspect of "fun." One day, my childhood friends and I climbed a steep cliff which rose above a stream near my house. It was a little dangerous, and we got tired, but it was a lot of fun.

[5] Another aspect of fun is that it often involves another person or a group of people. According to Webster's dictionary, "fun" originated from the old English word, "fonne," meaning "fool" or "foolish" or from "fonnen," meaning "to be foolish". "Foolishness" suggests that someone else must be present, as it is almost impossible to "be a fool" if no other people are watching you. This supports the fact that "having fun" usually involves another person or a group of people.

[6] "Fun" is a difficult word to translate.

Exercise 10

Imagine that your classmate asks you these questions about the essay. Write your advice.

Peer Advice Questions

A. Look at paragraph 2. How would you translate "fun" in your language? (In other words, what is the word for "fun" in your langage?)

B. Can you give me a sentence <u>in your language</u> using your expression for "fun"? Write the sentence in your language.

C. Translate into English the sentence that you just wrote in B above.

D. Look at the underlined words in paragraph 3. Should I say what the other language is and what the foreign word is? Why or why not?

E. Look at paragraph 4. Does this example help you understand "fun"? Why or why not?

F. Do you think I need more details to explain why this climbing was fun?

G. Describe an experience that you had that would help me explain "fun?"

H. Look at paragraph 5. Does this connection between "foolishness" and "other people" seem logical to you? Why or why not?

I. Do you agree that, to have fun, we always need other people? If you don't agree, please give me an example.

J. Look at paragraph 6. How can I improve my conclusion?

Grammar: *For practice with* **Conditional Sentences**, *do Grammar Unit 17.*

Exercise 11

Read the second draft of the essay below.

Is "Fun" an English-only Concept?

[1] The other day, I met my French friend who had just returned from vacation. When I asked him how his vacation had been, my friend (who is quite fluent in English) answered, "It was amusing."

Hearing that his vacation was just "amusing," I wondered what had gone wrong with it and said, "Oh, not very good, huh?"

He looked confused and responded, "No! Very good!"

The confusion in our conversation came from the English expression, "amusing." Since my French friend's vacation had been very good, he really needed to use the word "fun" to describe it. Instead, he used "amusing," which he had probably translated from the French expression, *"amusant."* The word "fun" needs clarification in order for non-native English speakers to truly understand it.

[2] Someone who studies foreign languages surely finds that certain expressions do not translate easily into other languages. For example, students of not only French, but also Japanese, would find that those languages lack exact translations for the English expression, "fun." This discovery might make one wonder whether, perhaps, other languages as well do not offer a direct translation for "fun." Is "fun" a uniquely English concept?

[3] "Fun" is such a common word in English that, as a student of French, I often wanted to use the French equivalent when communicating in French. French offers the expression, *"amusant,"* but the English equivalent, "amusing," does not quite match the meaning of "fun." In considering "amusant" (or "amusing" in English), board games, card games, and puzzles come to mind. "Fun," however, is not limited merely to man-made pastimes such as games.

[4] *"Tanoshi"* is often cited as a Japanese translation for "fun." However, in my dictionary *"tanoshi"* is actually translated as "cheerful" and "pleasant," which (just as with *"amusant"* in French) do not fit the exact meaning of "fun."

[5] One aspect of "fun" can be found by considering the (translated-from Japanese) expression, "cheerful." It is possible to say that an atmosphere of a place is cheerful, such as in, "The child's bedroom is cheerful." However, we would not say, "The child's bedroom is fun." This is because an aspect of "fun" is that it usually applies to enjoyable activities, rather than places.

(continued on the next page)

[6] Fun is generally associated with activities, but that is not the only aspect. The following episode introduces another important aspect of "fun."

[7] One day, my childhood friends and I climbed a steep cliff which rose above a stream near my house. It was not a very high cliff by adult standards, perhaps about 15 meters high, but for us 12-year-olds, it was a tough challenge. As we climbed, our hands moved carefully up, gripping protruding tree-roots or rocks. Each foot-hold also had to be carefully chosen. Step by step, as we forced ourselves up the vertical bare-dirt face of the cliff, our toes searched out roots and rocks to support our weight. Climbing only 15 meters up, we were never really in danger (even if we fell), but the stream below us was cold and uninviting. We eventually reached the top. Exhausted, we lay on the grass, gulping deep breaths of air, and resting our muscles as we waited for our strength to return.

[8] Surprisingly, in that experience, there was an important aspect of "fun." Someone might say that climbing a steep, dirty cliff, where (with each step) we risked falling into a cold stream, did not sound enjoyable at all.

[9] There was only one reason why we liked climbing that cliff that afternoon: we were entirely focused on it; in other words, that cliff absorbed our full attention. In fact, having one's total attention focused on the present moment is a second aspect of "fun." Our whole attention was on finding the next sturdy-looking support for our hands and feet. Time and our everyday problems were meaningless. We were having fun!

[10] A third aspect of "fun" can be found by considering the Japanese translation, "pleasant." In English, "pleasant" applies to quite mild experiences: for example, one can have a pleasant afternoon at home alone, but most people would probably not say that it is fun. Perhaps this is because "fun" often involves another person or a group of people.

[11] According to Webster's dictionary, "fun" originated from the Old English word *"fonne,"* meaning "fool" or "foolish," or from *"fonnen,"* meaning "to be foolish." "Foolishness" suggests that someone else must be present, as it is almost impossible to "be a fool" if no one else is watching. This reinforces the fact that "having fun" usually involves another person or a group of people.

[12] On the other hand, a person can have fun alone, too. Someone who is working at a hobby, e.g. building a model airplane or organizing a stamp collection, can be having fun. However, here it is necessary to return to the second aspect (mentioned above), that of concentrating totally on the present moment. If someone who is building a plane or organizing stamps becomes unaware of the passing of time, then that person is probably having fun.

[13] The father in my host family once told me, "If what you are doing isn't fun, stop doing it." I think that he was trying to tell me that I shouldn't be too serious all the time and to stop worrying. Now that I understand the word "fun," I realize that if I want to do something fun, I need to find an activity that is not only enjoyable but also that absorbs my attention. This seems like a good philosophy for life.

Exercise 12

Complete the outline of the second draft of "Is 'Fun' an English-only Concept?" on pages 74 and 75 by filling in the blanks in the outline below with the phrases from the box.

Paragraphs 1-3

___ from the French, "*amusant*."
___ Board games, card games, and puzzles are "amusing."
___ This essay will explain the
_X_ his vacation

Outline for "Is 'Fun' and English-only Concept

Working thesis: _____ expression "fun."

I. (paragraphs 1-2) Introduction

    A. My French friend said ___*his vacation*___ was "amusing."
        1. I was confused.
        2. He probably translated _____

II. (¶ 3) "*Amusant*" vs. "fun" (**Use similar term to compare and contrast.**)

    A. French speakers might mistakenly say "amusing" when they mean "fun."
    B. _____

Paragraphs 4-5

___ "cheerful" and "pleasant"
___ makes more sense than
___ "*tanoshi*"

III. (¶4-5) "Fun" usually refers to an enjoyable activity, rather than a person or place. (**Use negation.**)

    A. In Japanese, _____ is translated as "fun."
        1. However, they translate "*tanoshi*" as _____.
        2. "Cheerful" does not always equal "fun."
        3. "The child's bedroom is cheerful" _____
           "the child's bedroom is fun."

Paragraphs 6-11

___ fun activity

___ *"fonne"* meaning "fool," or *"fonnen"* meaning "to be foolish"

___ Fun often involves

___ was completely focused

IV. (¶ 6-8) Following is an example of a _____. **(Give an example.)**

   A. We climbed a steep cliff.

   B. It was dangerous, and we were exhausted.

V. (¶ 9-10-) There are two additional aspects of fun. **(Explain the parts.)**

   A. Our attention _____.

   B. _____ another person or a group of people.

VI. (¶ 11) Webster's Old English definition is _____

_____**(Tell the history.)**

Paragraphs 12-13

___ and absorbs

___ then stop doing it

___ alone

___ concentration

VII. (¶ 12) Fun can happen when we are _____. **(Give an example.)**

   A. Working at a hobby

   B. Total _____

VIII. (¶ 13) Conclusion: "If what you are doing isn't fun, _____."

(Quotation)

   A. Don't be too serious.

   B. The activity is enjoyable _____ my attention.

Extended Definition Essay, Style III: Define a Foreign Word That is Difficult to Translate (directly) into English.

Exercise 13

❶ Read the essay titled *"Salu"* below.

❷ Write the "Definition Strategy" that is used for each paragraph.

Strategies for Defining a Word

___ Give examples   ___ Explain parts   ___ Give the history

___ Use similar terms to compare and contrast   ___ Use negation

---

Salu

STRATEGY

INTRODUCTION
(no strategy used)

¹ Last night, on the evening news, I saw an interview with a teenager who had recently shot another youth. When asked why he had shot the boy, he said that it was because the boy had shown him disrespect. This report made me realize how universal the need for respect is. In fact, in my native language, Timberi*, we have a special word which is *salu,* and its unique characteristics make it difficult to translate directly into English.

_____

² The first time that someone called me a *salu* was when I was 18 years old. I was still living in my village at that time. A 13-year-old neighbor boy was having problems with some bullies, and he asked me for some help. We spent that entire afternoon together talking about his problem, some possible solutions, and life as a teenager. By the next week, the problem with the bullies was resolved. Ever since that day, he has called me by my name, Ken, and added the honorific *salu*: Ken-salu. He would also tell other people that I was his *salu.*

_____

³ *Salu* is a word that is impossible to translate directly into English. Some people think it means "teacher," but that is not accurate because many teachers are not called *salu.* In my high school, only five of our thirty teachers were called *salu.*

_____

⁴ Surprisingly, the word actually has a connection to English. About 300 years ago, there were English-speaking soldiers stationed in our country. These soldiers would greet each other with a salute by raising their right hand to their forehead as a sign of respect. *Salu* comes from "salute."

*Timberi is a fictitious language.

(continued on the next page)

5 In English, the word "mentor" has some similarities to *salu*. Like a mentor, a *salu* is always older than the other person. A mentor and a *salu* both give advice. However, it seems that for a person to be considered a mentor, the relationship has to continue for several months or even years. This is not necessary for a person to be a *salu*; the relationship can develop very fast, as it did with my neighbor. Even though we have never spent much time with each other since that one afternoon, he has continued to call me *salu*.

6 There are two important characteristics of a *salu*. One is that they helped someone learn something special. And, second, they continue to behave in a way that others will respect. As a result, once someone is considered a *salu* by someone else, there is pressure to perform well because it is possible to lose one's *salu* status. If my neighbor stopped calling me *salu,* I would be very troubled by it.

7 We can find *salu* in all parts of society. I call my computer-man *salu*; he not only sold me my first computer but also opened up the internet world to me through his instructions. Also, the mayor of our village is a *salu* to all our citizens. We chose him as our mayor because he was well repected. During the six years that he has been our mayor, he has never disappointed us.

8 Unfortunately, this special word is gradually changing in meaning. Over the past 30 years, our country has attracted immigrants whose native language is not Timberi. It is difficult for them to understand the true meaning of *salu,* so now almost all teachers are called *salu* by their students.

CONCLUSION 9 Most people in this world would like to be recognized and respected (no strategy used) by others. That may be the motivation for people to work hard to get advanced degrees, to run successful businesses, or do other good work. In my country, we are able to show our respect to special people, even to someone with nothing more than a lot of common sense, with the word *salu*.

Grammar: *For practice with* **Reduced Adjective Clauses***, do Grammar Unit 18 and Grammar Unit 19.*

☛ First draft assignment — Write the first draft

Exercise 14 Write an *Extended Definition Essay*.

❶ Choose a word as the topic of your essay. It can be one of these:

Possible Extended Definition Essay Topics

___ A common word in English

___ An English word that is difficult to translate
directly into other languages

___ A foreign word that is difficult to translate directly into English

Recommendations: Do not choose a physical word. It's difficult to use the strategies about something that is physical. Also, the ideas in your essay probably would not be unique or different from other students who wrote about that word. For example, "pedicab" (a three-wheel bicycle used as a type of taxi) and "sushi" are physical words that are not good for definition essays.

Option: If you yourself cannot find a word, you can use one of the words from Exercise 7.

---

❷ Write an outline or a first draft of an *Extended Definition Essay*.
❸ In your outline or first draft, identify the Definition Strategies that you used. (For example, see the list on p. 60, the outline for "Fun" on p. 76 or the essay *"Salu"* on p. 78.

Part 3: *Writing the second draft*

☛ Preparing to write the second draft
(Think about improving your first draft while you do these exercises:
◆ *Using sentence variety, p. 80;* ◆ *Writing for a specific audience, p. 85;* ◆ *Using peer-editing, p. 86)*

Strategy 6   Use a variety of sentence styles.

Exercise 15

❶ Read the essay titled "The Beatles" (Sample Text 1: boring style, on page 81) and look at the *subject* of each sentence (they are numbered).
❷ In the columns on the right, place a **X** next to each sentence's number to indicate whether it starts with the subject or does not start with the subject.

Exercise 16

❶ Read the essay titled "The Beatles" (Sample Text 2: varied style, on page 82) and look at the *subject* of each sentence (they are numbered).
❷ In the columns on the right, place a **X** next to each sentence's number to indicate whether it starts with the subject or does not start with the subject. (Six start with the subjects.)

Sample Text 1:
(boring style)

The Beatles

¹The Beatles had some unexpected turns "on their road to success" as one of the greatest rock bands in history. ²They were born in Liverpool, England, in the 1940's. ³They enjoyed music from a young age. ⁴George Harrison met Paul McCartney by chance on a school bus. ⁵They started talking about music and soon realized that they shared a love of it. ⁶Paul met John when Paul's friend forced him to go along to a neighborhood festival to see a band led by a kid named John Lennon. ⁷Paul was impressed by John's singing that night, so after the performance, he approached John and auditioned immediately for the band. ⁸John was impressed with Paul's talent too, so he asked Paul to join. ⁹John was confident of his own ability, so he was even willing to share the leadership of the band with this talented newcomer. ¹⁰Paul introduced the band to George Harrison, and he joined as well. (¹¹Ringo Starr joined some time later.) ¹²The threesome was eager to get a record contract, so they traveled on a freezing New Year's Eve to London for an important audition, but unfortunately they were rejected. ¹³That rejection could have broken the spirit of many bands, but the Beatles kept trying. ¹⁴They introduced themselves to George Martin. ¹⁵He was a record producer with no background in rock 'n roll. ¹⁶He signed a contract with them. ¹⁷Their first single was "Love Me Do." ¹⁸It made the "top 20" in England, but George Martin still did not have much confidence in the band's own songs. ¹⁹As a result, he found a song for the Beatles to sing called "How Do You Do It?" ²⁰The Beatles felt that that song had some weaknesses, so they rejected it. ²¹"Please, Please Me" was John's counter-proposal to "How Do You Do It?" and, in the end, it became a number-one hit. ²²The Beatles' songs began hitting the top of the charts on a regular basis, but, after a number of years, they lost interest in keeping the group together. ²³They split up at that point.

	Sentences starting with the subject *(of the sentence)*	Sentences *not* starting with the subject *(of the sentence)*
1	X	
2	X	
3		
4		
5		
6		
7		
8		
9		
10		
11		
12		
13		
14		
15		
16		
17		
18		
19		
20		
21		
22		
23		

Sample Text 2:
(varied style)

The Beatles

¹The Beatles had some unexpected turns "on their road to success" as one of the greatest rock bands in history. ²Born in Liverpool, England, they enjoyed music from a young age. ³When George Harrison met Paul McCartney by chance on a school bus, they started talking about music and soon realized that they shared a love of it. ⁴Paul met John when Paul's friend forced him to go along to a neighborhood festival to see a band led by a kid named John Lennon. ⁵Impressed by John's singing that night, Paul approached John after the performance and auditioned immediately for the band. ⁶John was impressed with Paul's talent too, so he asked Paul to join. ⁷Because of John's confidence in his own ability, he was even willing to share the leadership of the band with this talented newcomer. ⁸Paul introduced the band to George Harrison, and he joined as well. (⁹Ringo Starr joined some time later.) ¹⁰Eager to get a record contract, the threesome traveled on a freezing New Year's Eve to London for an important audition, but unfortunately they were rejected. ¹¹Although that rejection could have broken the spirit of many bands, the Beatles kept trying. ¹²After they introduced themselves to George Martin, a record producer with no background in rock 'n roll, he signed a contract with them. ¹³Despite the fact that their first single, "Love Me Do," made the "top 20" in England, George Martin still did not have much confidence in the band's own songs. ¹⁴As a result, he found a song for the Beatles to sing called "How Do You Do It?" ¹⁵Since the Beatles felt that that song had some weaknesses, they rejected it. ¹⁶"Please, Please Me," John's counter-proposal to "How Do You Do It?" in the end became a number-one hit. ¹⁷Though the Beatles' songs began hitting the top of the charts on a regular basis, after a number of years, they lost interest in keeping the group together. ¹⁸At that point, they split up.

	Sentences starting with the subject *(of the sentence)*	Sentences *not* starting with the subject *(of the sentence)*
1	X	
2		X
3		
4		
5		
6		
7		
8		
9		
10		
11		
12		
13		
14		
15		
16		
17		
18		

Exercise 17

Practice in Writing Sentence Variety

Rewrite these sentences in another style.

Note: The numbers on the right side of the page refer to the sentences in **Text 2 (varied style)** of "The Beatles" essay, page 82. Those sentences will help you decide what sentence style to use when you rewrite the sentences below.

In Text 2 (p.82), sentence:

a. Most Americans can afford to buy a variety of food at the supermarket, but many of them are not choosing healthy food.

11

Although most Americans can afford to buy a variety of food at the supermarket, many of them are not making healthy choices.

b. Many Americans are addicted to sugar, so they are eating more sweets than they should.

5

c. A sugar addict may think that they cannot live without sugar, but some experts say that a low-sugar diet increases energy and improves sleep.

13

d. Doctors are concerned about this sugar addiction, so they are telling their patients to be careful about what they eat.

7

e. Joe Potter tried to stop eating sugar, but he couldn't because he was addicted.   17

_____

_____

_____

f. Joe made a firm decision to stop eating sugar after reading a famous book entitled *Sugar Blues*.   12

_____

_____

_____

g. Joe continued his no-sugar diet for seven years, but he eventually gave in and began eating a lot of sugar again.   11

_____

_____

_____

h. Joe was discouraged that his addiction had returned, so he joined a self-help group for sugar addicts.   5

_____

_____

_____

i. He finally stopped eating sugar completely after sharing his experiences with other addicts in the self-help group.   12

_____

_____

_____

Grammar: *For practice with* **Adjective Clauses Reduced to Prepositional Phrases**, *do Grammar Unit 20.*

Writing for a Specific Audience: Type of Information and Style

Strategy 7   Think about your audience (the people who will read your essay).

Exercise 18

❶ For each of the paragraphs below, notice the *difference in style*.

❷ In each blank, write who the audience (the reader) is: (a) a *friend* or (b) a *teacher*.

AUDIENCE

_____ 1. The best way to spend next weekend is to start by going to Forest Park. I'll bet we'll be able to find some guys there who'll wanna play basketball.

_____ 2. The best way to spend a weekend is to start by going to Forest Park, which is a beautiful park covered with trees. It is sometimes possible to play basketball if enough people are available to make teams.

_____ 3. At first, he may have several questions, for example, how one can turn on the computer. This is, of course, the first basic step in the process.

_____ 4. So then he asked me stuff like how do you turn on the computer? And I'm like, wow! You don't even know that?

Exercise 19

❶ For both of the paragraphs below, notice the *difference in the type of information*.

❷ Tell whether the audience (the reader) is: (a) *your parents* or (b) *your best friend*.

AUDIENCE

_____ 1. One of the best features of this car is its size. We could easily fit six people inside: Johnny, you, me, and our girlfriends. Also, the engine is big, which will be good if we want to race it.

_____ 2. One of the best features of this car is its structure. It's built to be safe. For example, I read that, in an accident, the driver of this car is 75% less likely to have a serious injury than in other cars in its same class.

Exercise 20

❶ Choose <u>one topic</u> from the list below.

❷ Write a paragraph (about a half page) about the topic for *your parents* (or *teacher*).

❸ Write a paragraph (about a half page) about the *same* topic for *your best friend*.

Topics*

____ Explain why you want to quit school.

____ Describe your relationship with your boyfriend or girlfriend. (e.g. you can write the good and bad points, or you can write why you want to marry him or her.)

____ Tell about your plans for the future.

____ Tell about a mistake that you made, or something foolish that you did.

____ Explain why you are failing a course in school.

The information you write does not have to be true; you can use your imagination.

☛ **Second draft assignment — Write the second draft**

Exercise 21

Write a second draft of the *Extended Definition Essay* that you wrote on page 80.

Fluency Writing: **While working on your second draft, do a Fluency Writing from Section 2. After finishing the Fluency Writing, continue working on your second draft.**

Part 4: *Writing the final draft*

☛ **Preparing to write the final draft, using peer-editing**

Strategy 8   Get a reaction from a classmate.

Exercise 22: After you finish your second draft:

❶ Find some areas of the essay where you would like advice from another student. (*See sample on pages 72 and 73.*)
❷ On a different paper, write questions that you would like to ask.

Possible questions that you might ask to get advice

_____ Do you think I need more details here?
_____ Can you understand this sentence?
_____ Is this example helpful?
_____ Is this part interesting?
_____ Can you help me think of some details that I could use here?
_____ Do you think there is a grammar problem in this sentence?

Exercise 23

❶ Exchange essays with a classmate.
❷ Silently read your partner's essay.
❸ Point to the places on your essay where you would like advice and ask your questions. (*You do not have to make any changes to your essay if you do not want to.*)
❹ Also, answer your classmate's questions about their essay.

☞ Final draft assignment — Write the final draft

Exercise 24

Write a final draft of the *Extended Definition Essay* that you began on page 80. If you want, use some of the ideas that your peer-editing partner recommended.

Grammar: *For practice with* **Sentences with Initial Modifying Phrases,** *do Grammar Unit 21.*

To the teacher: see the *Teacher's Manual* for these photocopyable materials:
- **Definition Check-list**
- **Definition Evaluation Form**
- **Definition In-class Essay Topics**

Essay: *Extended Definition* • **Part 4:** *Writing the final draft* • **87**

Essay 4: Argumentation

(An argumentation essay explains the reasons for an opinion about a topic.)

Fluency Writing: Before starting this unit, do a Fluency Writing from Section 2. After finishing, begin working individually on the following exercises.

Part 1: *Focusing on the unique features*

Exercise 1: Read the sample essay, *"Choosing a Major,"* below.

**Argumentation:
Sample Essay 1**

Choosing a Major

¹ Choosing a major is one of the most important decisions that college students make. Once this decision has been made, the student's life will begin to move in a certain direction. At present, there are a large number of students at our community college with more than 30 credits (which equals about one year of full-time study) who have not chosen a major. There are, however, important reasons why the community college needs to either require indecisive students to choose a major or expel them.

² First of all, students who lack a goal and who spend three or four years at a community college are taking up space that more focused students could use. I am a Computer Science major who would like to get my degree in two years. Unfortunately, it is often difficult for me to find space in the Computer Lab. This is especially frustrating because old students (who have been in the college for 3 or 4 years) often take up space and use equipment that I need. These old students impede the progress of students like me who have chosen a major and are trying to graduate on time.

³ Second, it seems a waste of time for 20-year-olds to spend three or four years at a community college. It is obvious that most students in this situation need help from the college staff to them get focused, so that they can make a decision and give their life a direction. One of my classmates spent 4 years taking classes without a plan; finally, after talking to a counselor, he chose to major in Business Administration. Not surprisingly, many of the courses he had previously taken did not help him advance toward this degree, so he ended up wasting time and money.

⁴ Furthermore, according to the newspaper, our government officials are carefully looking at our community college since 75% of tuition costs are paid by taxpayers. As a result, college administrators are under pressure to explain why the enrollment is so high, yet the number of graduates has not increased. The underlying problem here is that too many students lack direction, which slows their progress toward graduation.

⁵ However, there are some students who disagree with me. One student told me that a lot of 18- and 19-year-olds do not know what their options for majors are, so they need to experience various courses in order to learn what their choices are. Nevertheless, I disagree with this opinion. By talking to counselors, instructors, and fellow students, within a few weeks, anyone should be able to get all the information that they need about the different majors and learn which one is best for them.

⁶ As community colleges become more and more popular, there is a greater need for administrators to make sure that college resources are used wisely. If students are required to choose their majors early and if they are helped to make wise decisions, everyone, including students, instructors, administrators, and taxpayers, will benefit.

Exercise 2: Use sentences in the box below to fill in the information about "*Choosing a Major.*"

_____ Administrators feel pressure from the tax-payers.

_____ Spending many years at a community college is a waste of time.

_X_ Students are taking up space.

_____ Students should not be forced to hurry and choose a major because some of them don't
     know what their options are and need to experience different courses.

_____ Students should choose a major or be expelled.

_____ Students can talk to counselors and others in order to get information on different majors.

Writer's position: _____

First support (for writer's position): *Students are taking up space.* _____

Second support: _____

Third support: _____

Other side's opinion: _____

_____

_____

Refutation (writer's response to the other side's opinion): _____

_____

Exercise 3: Answer these questions about the "*Choosing a Major*" essay on pages 88-89.

1. In which paragraph does the writer use information from a newspaper to support their opinion? _____
2. In which paragraph does the writer use a personal experience to support their opinion? _____
3. In which paragraph does the writer tell about the experience of someone else in order to support their opinion? ____
4. In which paragraph does the writer give an opposite opinion (i.e. the opinion of someone who disagrees)?____
5. In which paragraph does the writer explain weak points of the opposite opinion? ____

Grammar: *For a review of* **Commas and Semicolons**, *do Grammar Unit 22.*

Part 2: *Writing the first draft*
☛ Preparing to write the first draft

Exercise 4: Choose <u>two topics from the list</u> below and write <u>three arguments</u> of support for each topic. (Later, you might choose one of these two topics for your argumentation essay.)

Use This Format

Topic:
My opinion:
    Support 1:.
    Support 2:
    Support 3:

Example

Topic: Should the minimum drinking age be lowered to 18?
My opinion: The minimum drinking age should not be lowered from 21 to 18.
    Support 1: Young people cause accidents when they drink and drive.
    Support 2: Young people can more easily become alcoholics if they start drinking early.
    Support 3: Young people who drink cause social problems.

Possible Argumentation Essay Topics

1. Do you think it is a good idea for people to marry someone from a different country?

2. Do you think that mothers should stay home, rather than work outside their home, after they have children?

3. Should animals (for example, monkeys and rats) be used for research??

4. Should computer tablets replace textbooks in schools?

(name of city)

5. Do you think that marijuana should be illegal?

6. Do you think that our school should try to get more foreign students to attend here?

7. Before a couple is allowed to have children, should they be required to pass a "parenting course" that would teach them how to be good parents?

8. When elderly people become too old to live alone, should they live in a nursing home (i.e. old people's home) or with one of their children?

9. Which is a better age for getting married: 20 or 30?

10. If a couple has young children, should they stay married even if they are having marital problems, or should they separate?

11. Which is better: a family with only one child, or a family with four children?

12. Which is better: a roommate from your country, or one from a different country?

13. Should the death penalty be illegal?

14. Should owning a gun be illegal?

15. (Other topics: Tell your teacher before you start this assignment.)

Grammar: *For practice with* **Adjectives**, *do Grammar Unit 23.*

Exercise 5: In Exercise 4, you wrote support for two topics. In this exercise:

❶ Write the *other side's opinion* for both topics.
❷ Write <u>two arguments of support</u> for the other side's opinion for those two topics.

Use This Format

My opinion:

Other side's opinion:

   Other side's support 1:

   Other side's support 2:

Example

My opinion: *The drinking age should not be lowered to 18.*

Other side's opinion: *The drinking age should be lowered to 18.*

   Other side's support 1:
     If 18-year-olds are old enough to vote and serve in the military, they are old enough to drink.
   Other side's support 2:
     Liquor companies can make more money if 18-year-olds can drink.

Strategy 1 — Use a variety of ways to support your opinion.

Types of Support

_____ Personal experience (a story)
_____ Others' experience (a story)
_____ News
_____ Hypothetical situation
_____ Common knowledge

Exercise 6: Fill in the blanks below with the types of support in the box.

1. **Topic:** Should high school students have shorter summer vacations?
   My opinion: Yes, they should.
   Support: It was recently reported on TV that the test scores of high school students drop after summer vacation. According to the report, students tend to stop reading during the summer, which could explain the results. By having a shorter summer vacation, students' scores could improve significantly.

   (Type of support: _____)

2. **Topic:** Do you think it is acceptable to torture a terrorist who might have important information about a possible terrorist attack?
   My opinion: No, I don't think it is.
   Support: Most people would agree that torture is a terrible thing to do to anyone, even terrorists. Also, it is impossible to know whether the information that the terrorists tell us is the truth. They might make up stories just to make the torture stop.

   (Type of support: _____)

3. **Topic:** Is it best for a child to have at least one sibling (i.e. brother or sister)?
   My opinion: No, it is not best.
   Support: My best friend is an only child. His parents can afford to send him to an expensive music camp every summer. If he had siblings, his parents would not be able to afford this. In sum, if he had siblings, he probably wouldn't have been able to develop his musical talent as much as he has.

   (Type of support: _____)

4. **Topic:** Are online courses better than traditional ones?
   My opinion: Yes, they are.
   Support: Two years ago, I couldn't take a business class that I needed because my schedule during the day was too full, but there were no night classes. Therefore, I enrolled in an online course, and I loved it. I could study at any time of day, and I could do the assignments as fast or slow as I wanted. Moreover, it was easy to get answers to my questions because the professor was quick to respond to messages.

   (Type of support: _____)

5. **Topic:** Do you think people should drive their own cars, rather than use public transportation?

   My opinion: No, using public transportation is better.

   Support: Let's say that there is a businessman named Jim. To get from his house to work every day, it takes him 30 minutes by car or 40 minutes by bus. It would seem that a car is better. However, during the 40-minute bus ride, Jim can be productive by reading business reports or a newspaper, but in his car, he can only drive.

   (*Type of support:* _____)

Exercise 7: For <u>each</u> topic in the box below:

   ❶ Write your opinion.
   ❷ Write a paragraph of support.
   ❸ Tell the type of support you used from "Types of Support" from p. 92. (*For this exercise, your information does **not** have to be true.*)
   ❹ Try to use a variety of support.

Topics

1. Should women not work outside their homes after they get married?
2. Is spanking the best way to discipline a child?
3. Are pets good for families?
4. Do you think that people depend on their computers too much?
5. Should parents become their children's best friends?

Format for Exercise 7

Topic: _____
Your opinion: _____
Support: _____
Type of support: _____

Grammar: *For a review of* **Clauses and Phrases,** *do Grammar Unit 24.*

Strategy 2 Give the other side's support and then explain why it is not a good support.

Other side's support	**Expressions for Introducing the Other Side's Support** _____ Some people disagree with my opinion. _____ On the other hand, some people think . . . because . . . _____ Nevertheless, some people feel . . . They support their opinion by saying . . .

Refutation	**Expressions for Introducing the Refutation** *(writer's response to the other side's support)* _____ However, I disagree with their opinion. _____ My response to that argument is . . . _____ In response, I would say . . . _____ There is a problem with that argument.

Exercise 8: Fill in the blanks below with the phrases in the boxes.

Topic 1 Word Choices

_____ gives attention to the owner

_____ are independent and require less attention from

_____ their independence makes them less attractive

__x__ cats are better pets

Topic 1 **Writer's support**: _In my opinion, dogs are the best type of pet._ _____

Other side's support & refutation:

Nevertheless, some people feel that cats are better pets. They support their opinions by
(Expression for introducing the other side's opinion)
saying that _cats are better pets_ _____

_____ their owners

In response, I would say that _____
(Expression for introducing the refutaion)
_____as pets.

Most pet owners want a pet that needs them, likes attention and, in return, _____

_____

_____.

Topic 2 Word Choices

_____ I can hear the voices of people and the TVs

_____ are more enjoyable to listen to

_____ because they believe that

_____ late at night

Topic 2 **Writer's support:** _I feel that camping in a tent is better than staying in a hotel room._ _____

Other side's support & refutation:

On the other hand, some people think that staying in a hotel room is better _____

_____ it is quieter. However, I disagree with their opinion. In most

hotels that I have stayed in, _____ from the other rooms.

Often this noise continues until _____. However, the sounds

that I hear during camping are sounds of nature, which _____.

Topic 3 Word Choices

_____ running is better because runners can run at any time

_____ even after dark and when the weather is awful

_____ but they shouldn't because there is a chance that

Topic 3 **Writer's support:** _In my opinion, for exercise, swimming is better than running._ _____

Other side's support & refutation:

Some people disagree with my opinion. They say that _____

_____, but swimmers can swim only when the pool

is open. There is a problem with that argument. Runners may want to run after dark, _____

_____

they will get hit by a car or trip and fall. Also, it is dangerous to run during a storm. Nevertheless,

swimmers can get exercise _____.

❶ In the three boxes below, read the writer's opinion and their support.
❷ Write *Good* next to the good refutation, which clearly attacks the other side's support.
❸ Write *Not Good* next to the weak refutation, which does not mention the other side's support.

---

1. **Writer's opinion**: *I feel that living alone is better than having a roommate.*

   Other side's support: *Some people disagree with my opinion.* They say that, by having a roommate, we will feel more safe, especially at night. *My response to that argument is that. .*

   _____ a. roommates can be noisy, which can interfere with our studying.

   _____ b. by having good locks on our doors, we can feel secure even if we live alone. Also, a roommate might forget to lock a door, which could actually make us less safe.

---

2. **Writer's opinion:** *It seems to me that a community college is better than a large university for international students.*

   Other side's support: *On the other hand, some people think that* a university is better because, at most universities, students can rent inexpensive rooms in a dormitory on campus. In addition to being cheaper, they feel that this will make it more convenient for getting to class, and it will allow students more time to study. *There is a problem with that argument.*

   _____ a. For international students, university dorms have a few advantages, but they usually have many more disadvantages. For example, in dorms, students rarely have chances to cook their own food. By living off campus, which community college students do, they can cook for themselves and satisfy their desires for their own food.

   _____ b. For international students, having a small number of students in a class, which is more common at community colleges, is very important. They need to be able to feel free to ask questions of the instructor when they don't understand. Also, in small classes they will have more chances to make American friends.

---

3. **Writer's opinion:** *I believe that traveling by plane is better than by train.*

   Other side's support: *Nevertheless, some people feel that* trains are the better way to travel. *They support their opinion by saying that* on a train, passengers have a lot more room to spread their legs out and, in some cases, even lie down. *In response, I would say that . . .*

   _____ a. we will be more entertained on a plane because they often show movies.

   _____ b. we don't need a lot of leg room on a plane because our travel time is so short, compared to the time that we spend on a train.

Exercise 10

❶ Choose <u>three of the topics</u> in the box below and write paragraphs like those in Exercise 8 *(pages 94–95)*.

❷ Write a *brief* **argument for the other side** *(Use and underline the Expressions for Introducing the Other Side's Opinion, page 94.)* Include support for the other side's argument.

❸ Write a **refutation**. *(Use and underline the Expressions for Refutation, page 94.)* Explain the weak point of the other side's support (i.e. explain why you disagree with their support). *(See samples on page 96, paragraphs 1 to 3, and on page 89, paragraph 5.)*

Use This Format

Topic: _____

Your opinion: _____

_____

(Expression for introducing the other side's opinion and other side's support)

_____

_____

(Expression for introducing the refutation and the refutation)

_____

_____

Topics

1. **Topic:** Should students be allowed to eat in class?
2. **Topic:** Should families have only one, or more than one, child?
3. **Topic:** Should cigarette smoking be illegal?
4. **Topic:** Should young married couples live with their parents (in other words, with the wife's or husband's parents)?
5. **Topic:** Do social networks improve our relationships with other people?

Exercise 11

❶ Think of a topic.
❷ Write your opinion.
❸ Write the other side's argument and support.
❹ Write your refutation.

Exercise 12: Read this Argumentation sample essay, "Reasons Not to Lower the Drinking Age to 18."

Exercise 13: After reading the essay:

❶ Choose the **type of introduction** that is used in the essay.
   a. statistic   b. dramatic introduction   c. news

❷ In the essay, <u>underline</u> the **thesis statement**.

❸ Next to sections in **bold** print, fill in the blanks in the right margin with the **types of support** listed in the box.

Argumentation:
Sample Essay 2

Types of Support
_____ Personal experience
_____ Others' experience
_____ Hypothetical situation
_____ News
_____ Common knowledge

Reasons Not to Lower the Drinking Age to 18

TYPES OF SUPPORT

¹ It was Friday night after a busy week of classes. Tony decided to have a beer and relax with his friends. The only problem was that Tony was 19 years old, and the minimum legal age for drinking alcohol in Tony's state was 21. Thus, he and his friends drank secretly while parked in their cars on a deserted road in the countryside. After this get-together, they all drove home.

² Because Tony and his friends were forced to drive after drinking, it is obvious that minimum-age drinking laws have a weakness. Certainly, there are opponents, who think drinking-age laws are silly, but there are also supporters, who think they are necessary. I feel that it is absolutely necessary to have a minimum drinking age of 21, because, without it, young people and society in general would suffer a number of negative effects.

³ One negative effect of young people drinking is that they can cause accidents if they combine drinking and driving. **Of course, a drunken driver of any age is a danger on the road, but young people spend a lot of time driving around in cars. Young people also tend to be risk-takers, who can be easily influenced by their friends to drive fast and show off for others.** If we combine alcohol with immature, risky behavior, the likelihood of making a mistake while driving is increased even more. **In fact, it was recently reported that four young people were killed in an auto accident. The police discovered that all four, including the driver, had been drinking.**

Common knowledge

_____

⁴In addition to the destruction that can be caused by drinking and driving, a young drinker can suffer another kind of negative effect: the disease, alcoholism. **The Chicago Sun Times recently reported on a study which showed that consumption of alcohol can increase young people's chances of becoming addicted to alcohol.** Surprisingly, the study found that the younger people are when they begin drinking, the more likely they are to become alcoholics later in life. **Imagine that a 12-year-old boy is searching for a way to feel happy. A mature person will realize that people can get "high" naturally from physical exercise, walking in nature, or listening to music. However, an immature person like this boy, who does not understand "natural highs," may look for the fastest and easiest way to feel good. In some cases, this means that he will drink some alcohol. If drinking makes him feel good for a while, he probably will not search for pleasure through natural means. After six years of drinking, when he is only 18 years old, he may still know only one way of feeling happy: drinking alcohol.**

⁵However, there is more than just physical destruction that can be caused by drinking. Other types of negative effects can result as well, due to bad decision-making. **Most people would agree that if there is a noisy college dorm room on a weekend night, there is usually a beer-party going on in there.** Because of this noise, students living nearby who would like to study or go to bed are unable to do so. Recently, on our campus, 17 serious students moved out of the dorm because of loud weekend noise caused by drunken students. **I know, because I was one of them; I had gotten tired of the disturbances.**

⁶Furthermore, it is common for drunken students to start fights. **At the college which my brother attends, two gangs developed from a drunken fight that took place a while ago, and, now, unfortunately, the campus police are trying to control gang warfare, while innocent students try to attend classes and study.** Alcohol is at least partly to blame for this gang violence.

⁷**Also, drinking can cause poor judgment regarding sex.** This can result in unwanted pregnancies. Again, immaturity, risk-taking, and poor decision-making combined with alcohol can create problems that are hard, or impossible, to solve.

⁸ On the other hand, opponents of a minimum drinking age have their own position. Some say that, at least from the age of 18, young adults should be allowed to drink. They believe that, if 18- to 20-year-olds are mature enough to vote and to serve in the military, they should be able to drink legally. My response to that argument is that there seems to be little or no connection between the intelligence needed to vote for a good candidate or the physical ability needed to fight in a war and the capability to control oneself while drinking. Many 18-year-olds do not have enough experience with alcohol to know when they have drunk too much.

⁹ On top of that, people who think the drinking age should be lowered to 18 support their opinion by claiming that liquor companies can earn more profits if they can sell alcohol to 18-year-old people. They mistakenly believe that this would improve our economy. There is a problem with that argument. Our economy will actually suffer as a result of allowing young people to drink. Imagine that a young man named Peter starts drinking when he is 18. By the age of 20, he has become so addicted to alcohol that he needs to drink before going to work and during his lunch break. Because of this, he will be less productive and more likely to make costly mistakes or cause accidents. Now imagine thousands of workers who are just like Peter. It would be a catastrophe for our economy.

¹⁰ In conclusion, the reason why I chose this topic is because I have recently seen what can happen when young people drink. One of my friends who was a lot of fun to spend time with when she wasn't drinking would become violent when she was drunk. My roommate who was struggling to overcome his addiction to video games lost this battle when he started to drink. He now wastes most of his free time on these two addictions. Both of them are under 21 and drink illegally. If we lowered the drinking age to 18, there is no doubt that many more young people would face new challenges with breakdowns in relationships and with addictions.

Strategy 3 Write an outline to organize your ideas.

Exercise 13

Read the essay, "Reasons Not to Lower the Drinking Age to 18," on pages 98-100. Fill in the General Outline below with the words from the box.

Writer's opinion:
__ a good chance that they will make bad decisions __ apt to cause accidents
__ lowered to 18 __ more likely to become an alcoholic __ tend to be risk takers

Other side's opinion and Refutation:
__ actually suffer   __ 18   __ Liquor companies can
__mature   __ takes a certain kind of intelligence

General Outline
for "Reasons Not to Lower the Drinking Age to 18"

Writer's opinion: The drinking age should not be _____ .

Support 1: Young people _____ and when they
 drink and drive, they are _____.

Support 2: By starting to drink at an early age, a person is _____ .

Support 3: When young people drink, there is _____
_____ , for example, playing music too loudly,
getting into fights, and having unprotected sex.

Other side's opinion and Refutation

Other side's opinion: The minimum drinking age should be _____ .

Other side's support 1: If someone who is 18 can vote and serve in the military,
 it means that they are _____ .

Refutation 1: The ability to vote and to serve in the military _____
_____ that is different from the ability to control oneself
 while drinking.

Other side's support 2: _____ make more money,
 which can help the economy.

Refutation 2: The economy will _____ .

Essay: *Argumentation* • **Part 2:** *Writing the First Draft* • **101**

Strategy 4   Interview to get more support for your argument and the other side's argument.

Exercise 14

In Exercises 4 and 5 on pages 90 and 91, you chose two topics and wrote support for your side and for the other side. In Exercise 15, you will prepare to interview two people about one or both of those two topics and then interview them to get their opinions.

Sample interview questions

Topic: Should the minimum drinking age be lowered from 21 to 18?

Interview questions

1. Do you think the drinking age should be lowered to 18?

2. Can you give me reasons for your opinion?

3. Have you ever had any bad experiences with alcohol?

4. Do you know anyone who has had any problems (e.g. an accident or fight) because of alcohol?

5. If the drinking age were lowered, do you think it would affect your life?

6. Is there a law about a minimum drinking age in your country?

7. Would your parents get angry with you if you were under 18 and drank? If not, why not?

Exercise 15

Write 5 to 10 interview questions about one or both topics that you chose on pages 90 and 91.

Exercise 16

Interview two people about the topics. It's a good idea to take notes during the interviews. You can use their ideas if you want to, *but you are not required to.*

Grammar: *For exercises focusing on* **Word Choice Problems,** *do Grammar Unit 25.*

☛ First draft assignment — Write the first draft

Exercise 17: After you have chosen your topic from pages 90 and 91, you will fill in <u>one of these</u> general outlines before you write your essay.

General Outline, Option 1

Your opinion _____

Introduction

    Support 1 _____

    Support 2 _____

    Support 3 _____

    Support 4 (optional) _____

Other side's opinion _____

    Support 1 _____

    Support 2 _____

    Refutation of support 1 _____

    Refutation of support 2 _____

Conclusion: Explain why you think this information is important, or why you chose this topic.

General Outline, Option 2

Your opinion _____

Introduction

    Support 1 _____

    Support 2 _____

    Support 3 _____

    Support 4 (optional) _____

Other side's opinion _____

    Other side's Support 1 _____

    Refutation of support 1 _____

    Other side's Support 2 _____

    Refutation of support 2 _____

Conclusion: Explain why you think this information is important, or why you chose this topic.

Exercise 18

Write a first draft of an *Argumentation Essay* with the main ideas and some details. You should include:

1. A brief introduction and thesis statement

2. Three supports for your opinion
   Try to use some of these types of support to explain your opinion:

   - personal experience
   - others' experience
   - news
   - hypothetical situation
   - common knowledge

3. Two supports for the other side's argument. Try to use:
   - expressions for introducing the other side's opinion *(See page 94.)*

4. A refutation responding to the other side's supports. Try to use:
   - expressions for refutation *(See page 94.)*

5. A brief conclusion

   (For two sample essays, see pages 88-89 and pages 98-100.)

Part 3: *Writing the second draft*

☛ Preparing to write the second draft

(Think about improving your first draft while you do these exercises:
◆ *Writing an argumentation thesis statement, p. 105;* ◆ *Writing in an academic style, p. 106;*
◆ *Using peer-editing, p. 107)*

Fluency Writing: **While working on your second draft, do a Fluency Writing. After finishing the Fluency Writing, continue working on your second draft.**

Strategy 5   Write a clear argumentation thesis statement.

A **clear** thesis statement tells the reader *exactly* the side of the issue which you want the reader to agree with. It should be an opinion that people can agree or disagree with.

- **Weak thesis statement**: There are good points and bad points about renting an apartment. *(This is weak because it is not clear which side, the good points or bad points, you want the reader to agree with.)*

- **Good thesis statement**: Renting an apartment is better than buying a house.

Exercise 19

❶ Write **Good** next to the <u>five clear</u> thesis statements below.
❷ Write **Not Good** next to the <u>five weak</u> thesis statements.

_____ 1. Children with AIDS should be allowed to attend school with other children.

_____ 2. Permitting children with AIDS to attend school is a controversial issue.

_____ 3. Many people feel that we pay too many taxes. I will explain my opinion about this topic.

_____ 4. Our taxes should be reduced.

_____ 5. Children under the age of 13 who commit serious crimes should be treated like adults.

_____ 6. The proper treatment of children under the age of 13 who commit serious crimes is an important issue to consider.

_____ 7. When we start a job, many of us will decide to buy a car for transportation. However, it would be better for our society if citizens use public transportation rather than drive their own cars.

_____ 8. When we start a job, many of us will need to decide how to get to work. Some people like public transportation, but other people like using their own cars.

_____ 9. Eating in a restaurant, rather than eating at home, has advantages and disadvantages.

_____ 10. Eating in a restaurant is better than eating at home.

Strategy 6   Use an academic style.

Writing in an Academic Style	
PERSONAL STYLE	**ACADEMIC STYLE**
1. I think everyone likes spring.	1. Spring is *probably* one of the most popular seasons.
2. I believe that people watch too much TV.	2. *It seems that* people watch too much TV.
3. I feel community college students work too hard.	3. Community college students *seem to* work too hard.
4. I think children play with too many toy guns.	4. Children *tend to* play with too many toy guns.
5. I have noticed that college students are tired after a long day at school.	5. College students *look* tired after a long day at school.
6. I feel all college students should belong to clubs.	6. *It seems logical that* college students should belong to clubs.
7. I think even elderly people can contribute to society.	7. *Most people would agree that* even elderly people can contribute to society.
8. I was surprised that a large number of my classmates don't enjoy sports.	8. *A surprisingly large number* of my classmates don't enjoy sports.

Exercise 20

❶ Rewrite these sentences in a more academic style. *(See samples in the box above.)*
❷ <u>Underline</u> the expressions that you used to make the sentences more academic.

1. personal style: I feel college students need more free time.

   academic style: <u>*It seems that*</u> *college students need more free time.*

2. **p.s.:** I think that a healthy life style is very important for happiness.

   aca. style:

3. **p.s.:** I think young people should get advice about marriage before choosing a future spouse.

   a.s.:

4. **p.s.:** I believe that my friends spend more money on computer games than on clothes.

   a.s.:

5. **p.s.:** I have noticed that the average temperature in countries around the world has been rising.

   a.s.:

6. **p.s.:** I think college students are saving their money for school expenses since they don't wear fancy clothes.

   a.s.:

7. **p.s.:** I think tourists who shop at Duty Free Shops in airports buy things that they don't really need.
   a.s.:

8. **p.s.:** I was surprised that a large number of bullying incidents are causing problems in schools today.
   a.s.:

> **Grammar:** *For practice with* **Passive Voice**, *do Grammar Unit 26.*

☞ Second draft assignment — Write the second draft

Exercise 21
Write a second draft of the *Argumentation Essay* that you wrote on page 103.

Part 4: *Writing the final draft*

☞ Preparing to write the final draft, using peer-editing

Strategy 7	Get a reaction from a classmate.

Exercise 22

❶ Before doing this exercise, you may want to write another draft of your essay.
❷ *Choose one* of the peer-editing techniques below:

Technique 1: *Writer asks questions.*

❶ Write some numbers on your essay where you would like to ask a classmate for advice.
❷ On a piece of paper, write the questions that you would like to ask.

Technique 2: *Writer listens.*

Ask a classmate to read your essay to you aloud.

Grammar: *For practice with* **Reported Speech**, *do Grammar Unit 27.*

Exercise 23: Do the peer-editing technique that you chose in Exercise 22.

Technique 1: *Writer asks questions.*

❶ Find a partner.
❷ Give your essay to your partner and take your partner's essay.
❸ Read your partner's essay silently.
❹ Point to the places on your essay where you would like some advice and ask your questions. *(You do not have to make any changes to your essay if you do not want to.)*
❺ Reverse roles.

(or)

Technique 2: *Writer listens.*

❶ Find a partner.
❷ Give your essay to your partner and take your partner's essay.
❸ Your partner will read your essay silently first.
❹ Your partner will read your essay aloud to you. You can ask them to stop reading at any time and ask "peer-editing"-type questions.
❺ Reverse roles.

☛ Final draft assignment — Write the final draft

Exercise 24

Write a final draft of the **Argumentation Essay** that you began on page 104.
If you want, use some of the ideas that your peer-editing partner recommended. Also, try to:

* write a clear thesis statement. *(See page 105.)*
* use an academic style. *(See page 106.)*

To the teacher: see the *Teacher's Manual* for these photocopyable materials:
* **Argumentation Check-list**
* **Argumentation Evaluation Form**
* **Argumentation In-class Essay Topics**

Essay Unit 5: Essay with a Source and Mixed-Mode Essay

This unit is composed of two parts:
    Part 1. You will practice techniques for using a source in an essay.
    Part 2. You will practice techniques for writing an essay in which you use a different mode (e.g. narration, exposition, argumentation, or definition) in each paragraph.

Part 1: *Using a source in an essay*

In this part, you will practice how to write an essay in which you use information from a source (an article). You will practice the "sandwich technique," which is an academic way to organize information in this type of essay. In this technique, *every paragraph of the body* of your essay will have these features:

1. a topic sentence
2. a quote from the source (an article)
3. a brief explanation of what the quote means
4. an explanation of how the quote is connected to your thesis statement (or topic sentence)

Part 1a: Article, "Understanding Conformity," and sample essay using the sandwich technique

    First, you will read the following article, "Understanding Conformity," and complete some exercises about it. After that, you will read and analyze a sample essay which uses the sandwich technique and includes information from this article, "Understanding Conformity." Finally, you will read another article and write an essay using this technique.

Exercise 1: Read the article, "Understanding Conformity."

Understanding Conformity
David Kehe

¹ Shortly after I turned sixteen, my father started to hate me. At least, that is how I felt. It began with my hair, which was growing over my ears. Suddenly, we were no longer buddies, talking about baseball and laughing at stories that we told each other at dinner. I was treated like an outsider who had moved into his home.

² It took twenty years for me to understand what really had happened between us. The animosity he felt toward me has subsided, softened by the passage of time. Nevertheless, we have never recovered the bond between us that we had enjoyed before my hair divided us.

³ To my father, my hair style was a rejection of his values. In other words, I was not conforming to his world. He could not understand why I wanted to be different. However, in my mind, I was not trying to

be different; instead, I was just trying to be the same as the people whom I saw in my future—my generation. Ironically, I suppose that I was a non-conformist and a conformist at the same time.

[4] When people discuss conformity, they are also talking about expectations. For my father, one expectation was that if you are a male, you should have short hair. If people conform to certain expected standards, others will know what kind of person they are, and they will be able to anticipate what kind of relationship they will have. It is a kind of "shortcut" to knowing someone. But if someone dresses or behaves differently, it is sometimes hard to even know where to begin to understand another person. I can clearly recall the first time that I met a Muslim person who was dressed in a robe at a party. After the host introduced us to each other, I had no idea about what to say.

[5] People tend to act in a certain way in order to get some type of reward or to avoid a punishment. A man who is interviewing for a job in a bank may have a better chance of being rewarded with a job offer if he wears a tie that is similar to the ties that the regular bank employees wear. The opposite result would probably happen if the man wore the same style of tie when interviewing for a job as a drummer in a rock band.

[6] Of course, the easiest thing to do is to conform to the values of groups of people whom you are automatically associated with—your parents, your neighborhood friends, and your classmates. The bravest people are those who choose *not* to conform because they have discovered new values. It takes a lot of courage and strength to do something on your own that *you* have decided is right for you and not what *someone else* has decided is right for you. However, the risk is that you will no longer benefit from the security of knowing what to expect from those people with whom you had conformed in the past.

[7] As I look back on my father's reaction to my over-the-ears hair style, I realize that it probably was not hatred that he felt but rather the pain of loss. I think he suddenly realized that I was going to be different for him and that the son he once knew would no longer exist. He was going to have to learn to understand this new person.

This will be the "Source Cited":
Kehe, D. (2015). Understanding Conformity. *Writing Strategies: Advanced.* Brattleboro, VT: Pro Lingua Associates.

Exercise 2

Answer these questions about the article "Understanding Conformity." Write T (true) or F (false) in the blanks.

___ 1. The writer and his father had a close relationship until he turned 16.

___ 2. The father was happy that the writer was independent and different from the father.

___ 3. According to paragraph 4 (¶ 4), if you behave the way people expect you to, they will be confused.

___ 4. In ¶ 5, it says that you might get a reward or punishment according to how you dress. It depends on the situation.

___ 5. According to ¶ 6, it takes a lot of courage to choose by yourself how you should behave.

___ 6. In sum, the author thinks that people should always conform to others.

Exercise 3

In your essay, you will choose some sentences from the article to quote and to explain what they mean. Advanced writers write explanations of a quote which explain the deeper meaning with different words. Low-level writers write simple explanations which just repeat the words in the quote.

❶ Write "advanced" next to the deep explanations of the quotes.
❷ Write "low level" next to the simple explanations of the quotes.

1. From ¶ 2: "The animosity he felt toward me has subsided, softened by the passage of time."

____advanced____ a) After a few years, the father stopped feeling angry at his son, the writer. The father may have realized that what he was angry about probably wasn't very important.

____low level____ b) The anger that the father felt toward the son subsided and became soft as time passed.

2. From ¶ 3: "To my father, my hair style was a rejection of his values."

_____ a) Because my hair style was different from his, my father thought that I didn't accept his values. He thought my values had become different.

_____ b) Because my hair style was different from his, my father and I had a conflict. He believed that we no longer had similar ideas about what was important in life.

3. From ¶ 5: "People tend to act in a certain way in order to get some type of reward or to avoid a punishment."

_____ a) People behave so that they can get rewards or so that they don't get punishments. This is because rewards are good, and punishments are not.

_____ b) People are motived by rewards and punishments. They will direct their actions in ways that will increase rewards and decrease punishments.

Essay: *Essay with a Source* • **Part 1:** *Using a Source in an Essay-* • 111

Strategy 1   Use the sandwich technique.

Sample essay using sources

Exercise 4

Read the essay, "The Conformity Decision," on the next page and fill in the blanks with words from the box below.

Paragraphs 1-3

- the article, Kehe (2015) discusses
- increased their chances of being successful
- What is important is that we ourselves make
- to avoid a punishment" (p. 110). Basically, Kehe is saying that
- reading the article, "Understanding Conformity," I concluded that
- The author suggests that people
- life, it means that they

Paragraphs 4-5

- Kehe also points out that if
- It is important that college
- *Writing Strategies*
- example, a year ago, I was feeling
- I agree with Kehe. On top of that, I would
- easier to make decisions
- In his opinion, it is

Exercise 5

The right column on the next page is labeled "Parts of the essay." Fill in the blanks in the essay with the words in the box below.

- ✔ • thesis statement
- ✔ • 1st quote
- • explanation of 1st quote
- • relating 1st quote to thesis statement about "success"
- • 1st topic sentence
- • 2nd quote
- • explanation of 2nd quote
- • relating 2nd quote to thesis statement about "success"
- ✔ • 2nd topic sentence

The Conformity Decision

	Parts of the essay

1) When young people are about to leave home, whether to go to college or to get a full-time job, they tend to encounter a variety of pressures. One of the pressures that they might experience is to conform to certain standards of dress or behavior. Young people who like to wear casual clothes may have to dress more formally if they work in an office. A college student who prefers to sleep late in the mornings but work late at night might have to conform to a different schedule in order to take required classes at college. After _____ _____ to be successful in life, it doesn't matter whether we conform or not conform to a certain standard. _____ _____ the decision. — *thesis statement*

2) When someone is successful in _____ _____ are living in a way that helps them accomplish their goals. Someone's goals might be to make a lot of money, have an interesting job or avoid stress. In fact, there are different techniques that people use to become successful. One of these techniques is to conform to the standards that are commonly accepted. Another technique is to not conform.

3) In _____ people's motivation for their behavior. He states, "People tend to act in a certain way in order to get some type of reward or _____ — *1st quote* _____ if we behave the way a group of people wants us to, we may be able to get something we want. For example, if a boy wears clean clothes, he may be able to get a date with a girl who expects that characteristic in a boy. _____ _____ can also avoid a negative event by acting in a way that people expect. If a police officer stops a driver for speeding and if the driver uses polite language, the officer might not give him a ticket. In both of these cases, the boy who wants a date and the driver who was speeding made a decision to conform to what someone else would expect. By doing this, they _____ _____ in their goal.

4) It is also possible to be successful by not conforming. In fact, Kehe observes, "The bravest people are those who choose not to conform because they have discovered new values" (p. 110). _____ _____ usually easier to just behave and dress the same as other people around us. This is because we don't have to make any decisions; we just follow. We may feel comfortable because we tend to feel that if most people are doing something, it must be the right thing to do. _____ _____ we notice that the actions of others don't feel right to us, it will take a lot of effort to behave in a different way. _____ _____ add that even though it takes strength, if we truly believe that a different way is best for us, we will feel successful only if we choose to follow the new way. For _____ _____ pressure to conform to my parents' wishes. They wanted me to get a job and start a family, just like my brothers and sisters did. However, my goal in life is to have a lot of different experiences, and I knew that I couldn't be successful in this goal if I started a family. Thus, I didn't conform, and now I feel satisfied with my decision.

5) _____ _____

_____ students seriously consider their goals in life. Without clear goals, they are apt to mindlessly conform to whatever their peers are doing. This can mean wasting time pursuing pleasures, like playing video games or taking drugs. Most students with clear goals will see that those types of pastimes will not help them become successful. After students' goals are established, it is _____ _____ about which standards they want to (or need to) conform to and which ones they don't.

Source Cited

Kehe, D. (2015) Understanding Conformity. _____ _____ *Advanced*. Brattleboro, VT: Pro Lingua Associates.

2nd topic sentence

_____

_____

_____
_____
_____

Part 2b: Article, "Characteristics of Addiction" and essay assignment

In this section, you will read the article, "Characteristics of Addiction." Then, you will complete a study guide, choose a topic and write an essay using the sandwich technique with information from the article.

Purpose of this assignment: Are you addicted to something, for example, the Internet, cell phones, chocolate, or shopping? You will write an essay explaining why you think you are, or are not, addicted to something. You will use information from the article, "Characteristics of Addiction," to support your opinion.

Exercise 6: Read the article, "Characteristics of Addiction."

Characteristics of Addiction
Peggy Dustin

[1] In the movie, *Owning Mahowny*, a true story about a gambling addict, the main character, Dan Mahowny, seemed to make an endless number of bad decisions. He had an important position in a bank, so he was able to secretly take money from accounts; this money that he "took" (in fact, that he stole) supported his gambling habit. Throughout the movie, the audience is tempted to yell at him, "Stop it!" When he lost money on bets, he would "borrow" (in essence, steal) more money from the accounts at his bank in order to bet more money with the hope of winning enough to pay back the money he had stolen. If he lost, he "borrowed" even more money from those accounts. If he won, he continued to gamble even more. One time, he was in Las Vegas with over one million dollars that he had taken from his bank. He started out lucky, and eventually, he was ahead by $9 million. The movie audience is hoping that he will stop, but he doesn't. After gambling all night, he lost all of the $9 million. In the end, he was caught by investigators and went to prison for stealing over $10 million from the accounts at his bank. It became clear that Mahowny was addicted to gambling and that it ruined his life.

[2] Often, when we think about addictions, our minds conjure up images of people taking destructive drugs like heroin, or drinking alcohol or gambling. We can clearly see that these are ruining people's lives and that their behavior seems completely irrational. We want to shout, "Quit it!" Fortunately, most of us don't have serious addictions such as to drugs, alcohol, or gambling, but we may still engage in other types of "addictive" activities that might motivate an observer to yell, "That's enough!" These activities can range from doing too much physical exercise, to obsessively reading the news, to spending too many resources (time and money) on traveling. Scientists describe these addictions as a powerful desire to engage in an activity, even when it produces negative consequences.

[3] People with any kind of addiction believe that their regular everyday life is missing something. They overdrink, use dangerous drugs or perhaps spend excessively on travel or on shopping because these activities give them a "high" which they cannot normally find in ordinary life. It might start as a pleasurable experience, but it turns into an addiction when the person doesn't feel

normal without it. While engaging in the activity, the addict feels that everything in life is better than normal, and that life is, in fact, quite enjoyable!

[4] Another aspect of an addiction is that the addict will lose interest in daily activities. Talking to friends or family members doesn't seem very stimulating. There is a great temptation to avoid study or work. As a result, the addict might experience communcation breakdowns in relationships and become irresponsible about their homework at school or duties at work.

[5] Addicts frequently develop obsessive thoughts about their addiction. Early in the day or while engaged in some other activities, an alcoholic, for example, will probably start thinking about when the next opportunity to have a drink will arise. I went on a trip to Hawaii with some friends, including one who had a drinking problem. One day, we were visiting a spectacular waterfall. Thanks to the late-afternoon sun, the light was shining on the water in a unique way, which left all of us in awe—except for one of my friends. He was impatiently urging us to hurry up and take some photos so that we could return to our hotel. When we finally did return there, within five minutes, he had a drink in his hand. It is sad to think that he had probably been more focused on getting his next drink than on the beauty of the waterfall.

[6] Is it possible that common daily activities can become addictions that have characteristics that are similar to dangerously-addictive substances like drugs? In fact, anything that someone becomes obsessed with and that interferes with the things that that person really needs to do, such as paying attention to friends, family members, school, and work, can be considered an addiction. Let's next consider someone who enjoys watching sports.

[7] There is a common agreement that an addiction can have a negative impact on the addict's life. For many people, watching sports is just a pleasurable way to spend time. However, for sports-watching addicts, it can interfere with their ability to engage in pastimes that are more productive. For example, instead of getting physical exercise, sports-watching addicts may spend a whole weekend in front of the TV watching one game after another. Instead of enjoying dinner with their family, they mindlessly shovel their food into their

mouths while their attention is entirely focused on a game. From the article's point of view, meaningful conversations become impossible because social interactions create obstacles that trigger feelings of frustration.

[8] Another common characteristic is a tendency to become angry if someone suggests that the addict is losing control of his life. The sports-watching addict may lash out in anger at someone who turns off the TV in the middle of a game. For most addictions, the addicts feel that they "can stop" any time that they want. Ironically, however, one addict explained the true nature of the condition like this: I can give up my addiction, as long as I can wait until next Tuesday.

[9] These addicts may defend themselves by strongly denying that they are, for example, watching sports too much. In fact, addicts are

seldom aware of how much time they are devoting to their favored pastime. The sad reality is that they have little sense of how much time has passed while they are engaged in the activity.

[10] Deep inside themselves, many addicts realize that they could improve the quality of their lives if they spent more time focusing on other aspects of life that are more meaningful. Instead of watching sports all day, the addict knows that reading a book or interacting with others would be a more fruitful use of time. Yet, at the same time, the sports-watching addict feels he will miss something extremely thrilling if he isn't constantly watching. Ironically, the extreme thrills might not happen often enough, or the thrills might not be exciting enough; this can result in a sense of dissatisfaction and, in turn, a hunger to watch even more sports.

[11] For those without an addiction, it can be difficult to understand why someone would prefer to live a life in which one's mind is not focused on reality. Actually, as with other addictions, the sports-watching addicts are not addicted to the activity, but instead, are addicted to *the mood that they experience* when they are engaged in the activity. Many people who are addicted to a certain behavior, such as sports-watching or shopping, feel a "high" from the adrenaline that is released when they do that activity. The addiction can be a way of dealing with emotions such as boredom, stress, or loneliness. Unfortunately for the addicts, even when they are not necessarily feeling bored, stressed, or lonely, there is a temptation to participate in the activity.

_____

You can use this as your citation for this source:

Dustin, P. (2015). Characteristics of Addictions. *Writing Strategies: Advanced*. Brattleboro, VT: Pro Lingua Associates.

Exercise 7

From the article, "Characteristics of Addiction," make a list of the characteristics of an addiction. (It's acceptable to quote from the article for this exercise.) Below are two characteristics. Find at least <u>four</u> more.

1) (In paragraph 2) "Scientists describe these addictions as a powerful desire to engage in an activity, even when it produces negative consequences."

2) (In paragraph 3) "People with any kind of addiction believe that their regular everyday life is missing something."

3) _____

   _____

4) _____

   _____

5) _____

   _____

6) _____

   _____

Optional: You can add more to the list above.

Essay: *Essay with a Source* • **Part 1:** *Using a Source in an Essay-* • **117**

Strategy 2	Introduce a quote and explain it deeply

Exercise 8

❶ Read the quotes below.
❷ Look at the quotes in numbers 3-8 again and choose four of them.
❸ Copy the four quotes that you chose and write advanced explanations of them. (Write on another piece of paper.)

Note: Ignore the underlines until Exercise 10 and 11.

1. **Example** Quote from ¶ 8: <u>Dustin states</u>, "Another common characteristic is a tendency to become angry if someone suggests that the addict is losing control of his life" (p. 114).

   Low-level explanation: *The author is saying that addicts tend to get angry if anyone says that they don't have control of themselves.*

   Advanced explanation: *<u>The author is saying</u> that the addicts believe that they are living a normal life and are able to manage the activity that they are enjoying. If someone points out to them that this is not true, the addicts may become irritated at the person for suggesting that. They believe that other people cannot really know how they feel.*

2. **Example** Quote from ¶ 11: <u>The article reports</u>, "The addiction can be a way of dealing with emotions such as boredom, stress or loneliness" (p. 117).

   Low-level explanation: *Dustin believes that when addicts don't feel that life is comfortable or interesting, they will participate in their addictive activity.*

   Advanced explanation: *<u>Dustin believes</u> that addicts tend to use their addictive behavior to escape negative feelings. If, on occasion, they have nothing to do or no one to spend time with, they will fill up the time with the addictive activity.*

3. Quote from ¶ 2: The author observes, "Scientists describe these addictions as a powerful desire to engage in an activity, even when it produces negative consequences" (p. 115).

   Low-level explanation: *According to the article, addicts feel a strong need to participate in the addictive behavior. They tend to ignore negative results.*

   Advanced explanation: (Write on other paper.) *<u>According to the article,</u> ...*

4. Quote from ¶ 3: Dustin observes, "People with any kind of addiction believe that their regular everyday life is missing something" (p. 115).

   Low-level explanation: *In the author's opinion, people with addictions are not happy with their life because something is missing for them.*

   Advanced explanation: (Write on other paper.) *In the author's opinion, ...*

5 Quote from ¶ 4: Dustin states, "Another aspect of an addiction is that the addict will lose interest in daily activities" (p. 116).

> **Low-level explanation**: *This means that people who have addictions will not enjoy things that they do every day.*

> **Advanced explanation**: (Write on other paper.) *This means that …*

6 Quote from ¶ 6: The author argues, "In fact, anything that someone becomes obsessed with and that interferes with the things that that person really needs to do … can be considered an addiction. " (p. 116).

> **Low-level explanation**: *In other words, Dustin believes that if an activity interferes with important things in your life and you are obsessed with it, you are probably addicted to it.*

> **Advanced explanation**: (Write on other paper.) *In other words, Dustin believes that …*

7 Quote from ¶ 8: The author mentions that one addict explained, "… I can give up my addiction, as long as I can wait until next Tuesday" (p. 116).

> **Low-level explanation**: *Basically, Dustin is saying that addicts can stop their addictive activity next Tuesday.*

> **Advanced explanation**: (Write on other paper.) *Basically, Dustin is saying that …*

8 Quote from ¶ 10 : The article claims, "Deep inside themselves, many addicts realize that they could improve the quality of their lives if they spent more time focusing on other aspects of life that are more meaningful" (p. 117).

> **Low-level explanation**: *The author's point is that addicts understand that their lives could improve if they focused on more productive aspects.*

> **Advanced explanation**: (Write on other paper.) *The author's point is that …*

Exercise 9 (Write on other paper.)

❶ Find <u>two</u> more quotes from the article.
❷ Write the quotes.
❸ Write *advanced explanations* of the quotes.

Strategy 3   Use academic expressions to introduce a quote.

Exercise 10: You will use these expressions in your essay.

❶ Look at the quotes in Exercise 8 again.

❷ Make a list of the expressions for introducing a quote.

Expressions for introducing a quote

1. Dustin states, "..."   5. _____

2. The article reports, "..."   6. _____

3. _____   7. _____

4. _____   8. _____

Strategy 4   Use academic expressions to introduce an explanation of a quote.

Exercise 11: You will use these expressions in your essay.

❶ Look at the explanations of the quotes in Exercise 8 again.

❷ Make a list of the expressions for introducing explanations of the quotes.

Expressions for introducing the explanation of a quote

1. The author is saying that ...   5. _____

2. Dustin believes that ...   6. _____

3. According to the article, ...   7. _____

4. _____   8. _____

Exercise 12: Fill in the blanks with the correct form of "addict."

Noun	Adjective
• addict (a person)	• addictive
• addiction	• addicted [addicted to ___]

1. My friend smokes a lot. In fact, he is _____ to cigarettes.

2. The nicotine in tobacco is _____ . This chemical gives the smoker a "good" feeling.

3. Ken would like to quit smoking. However, he realizes that he is an _____ , so it is difficult for him to quit.

4. Cigarettes cost a lot, so it is an expensive _____ .

5. Some _____ enjoy their _____ so much that they don't want to stop.

6. If we can't stop using (or doing) something, we might become _____ to it.

Discussion of *Characteristics of Addiction*
Student A

Exercise 13

❶ You will be in a group of three or four students of Students A, B and C.

❷ Read these questions to Students B and C and answer theirs.

1. In ¶ 2, the author talks about some activities that people can become addicted to, besides drugs, alcohol and gambling. What are three activities that she mentions?

4. This question is connected to ¶ 4. All of us should answer this. Do you have an activity that is more enjoyable than daily activities? What is the activity?

7. Re-read ¶ 7 again for one minute.

10. Look as the last sentence in ¶ 8. Explain what the author means in the sentence, "I can give up my addiction, as long as I can wait until next Tuesday."

13. This question is connected to ¶ 10. All of us should answer this. Is there an activity that gives you a special thrill?

16. Let's check our answers for Exercise 12 on page 120.

Discussion of *Characteristics of Addiction*

Student B

Exercise 13

❶ You will be in a group of three or four students of Students A, B and C.

❷ Read these questions to Students A and C and answer theirs.

2.   In ¶ 3, the author says that an addictive activity gives people a "high"? Describe a "high" that people can feel from an activity.

5.   In ¶ 5, the first sentence mentions "obsessive thoughts." Explain the phrase "obsessive thoughts" in your own words, or tell me an example.

8.   Without looking at ¶ 7, describe how the sports-watching addiction can have a negative impact on the addict's life.

11.   Explain the last sentence in ¶ 9.

14.   This question is connected to ¶ 11. All of us should answer this. Is there an activity that you like to do when you are feeling bored, stressed or lonely? Explain.

Discussion of *Characteristics of Addiction*

Student C

Exercise 13

❶ You will be in a group of three or four students of Students A, B and C.

❷ Read these questions to Students A and B and answer theirs.

3. This is a discussion question. All of us should answer this. Tell me about an activity that gives you a high feeling. Describe the feeling that you get when you are doing that activity.

6. This is a discussion question. All of us should answer this. Do you have obsessive thoughts about something?

9. This is a discussion question. All of us should answer this. Do you do an activity that has a negative impact on your life? Explain.

12. This is a discussion question. All of us should answer this. Do you have little sense of time when you are doing an activity? Explain.

15. This is a discussion question. All of us should answer this. After reading this article, do you think that you are addicted to a certain activity? Explain.

☞ Preparing to write the first draft

Exercise 14

Essay Assignment: Addictions

Think of an activity that you enjoy doing, for example, shopping, eating certain food, sending messages, watching movies, doing puzzles, watching sports, playing video games, using your phone, spending time with your boyfriend or girlfriend, etc.

Imagine that your friend says to you, "I think that you are addicted to (an activity)." Write an essay explaining why you agree or disagree with your friend. In your essay, refer to the characteristics of addiction from the article "Characteristics of Addiction" on pages 115-117.

Before you write the complete essay, you should do **Exercise 15** first.

Organization of your essay:

1) Write an introduction and thesis statement.
2) Write 2-5 paragraphs of support for your thesis. In each of the paragraphs, you should:
   [1] start with a topic sentence. The topic sentence should be about addictions in general, not about your specific addiction.
   [2] include a quote from the article by Dustin. You should introduce the quote with one of the expressions. (See Exercise 10 above.)
   [3] explain what the author means by that quote. You should introduce the explanations with one of the expressions. (See Exercise 11 above.)

   [4] relate the quote to your thesis statement or topic sentence.
3) Write a conclusion. You should do at least one of these:
   -explain why this information is important.
   -explain what you have learned about yourself from writing this essay.

   -give a recommendation to other people.
4) Include "Source Cited" at the end.

Your thesis statement can be one of these:

- My friend says that I am addicted to _____. After reading "Characteristics of Addiction," I agree. *(Note: You can make up an addiction.)*

- My friend says that I am addicted to _____. After reading "Characteristics of Addiction," I do not agree. *(Note: You can make up an addiction.)*

- After reading "Characteristics of Addition," I think that _____ is addicted to _____. *(name of friend, relative)* *(Note: You can make up an addiction.)*

(Look at "The Conformity Decision" for a sample essay.)

Strategy 5	Write the first paragraph of the body first.

Exercise 15

Before you write your complete essay, you will write just the <u>first paragraph</u> of the body of your essay.

Do these steps and put a check mark (✓) in each of the boxes.

☐ 1) Write your thesis statement at the top of your paper. DO NOT write your introduction.

☐ 2) Choose your first quote, but don't copy it yet.

☐ 3) Write the topic sentence of the first paragraph of the body. The topic sentence should be about addictions in general, not about your specific addiction. The idea of this sentence should be connected to your first quote. (Look at Essay with a Source: The Sandwich Technique, "The Conformity Decision" Exercise 5.)

☐ 4) Introduce the quote. (See Exercise 10.)

☐ 5) Write the quote.

☐ 6) Write the citation after the quote.

☐ 7) Explain what the quote means.

☐ 8) Relate the quote to your thesis statement.

☐ 9) Show your paragraph to your instructor before you start to write your complete essay.

Exercise 16: Write the first draft of your essay.

Strategy 6	Get a reaction from a peer.

Peer Editing Check-list

My name is _____

My peer-editing partner is _____

Exercise 17

❶ Silently read your peer-editing partner's essay.

❷ Re-read the essay and answer these questions.

1. Did the essay have a clear thesis statement? _____

2. Look at the first paragraph of the body.

    a) Does it have a topic sentence? _____

    b) Is the topic sentence about <u>addiction in general</u> or about a <u>specific addiction</u>? (Choose one.)
(It should be about addiction in general.)

    c) Does the topic sentence include the quote? _____ (The answer should be NO.)

    d) Does the writer introduce the quote with a phrase, for example, "according to the author"? ___

    e) Does the writer cite the source after the quote? _____

    f) Does the writer explain the meaning of the quote? _____

    g) Does the writer relate the quote to his/her thesis statement? _____

2. Look at the second paragraph of the body.

    a) Does it have a topic sentence? _____

    b) Is the topic sentence about <u>addiction in general</u> or about a <u>specific addiction</u>? (Choose one.)
(It should be about addiction in general.)

    c) Does the topic sentence include the quote? _____ (The answer should be NO.)

    d) Does the writer introduce the quote with a phrase, for example, "according to the author"? _____

    e) Does the writer cite the source after the quote? _____

    f) Does the writer explain the meaning of the quote? _____

    g) Does the writer relate the quote to his/her thesis statement? _____

3. Look at the end of the essay.

    a) Are the words "Source Cited" centered? _____

    b) Is the form for the source correct? _____

    c) Is the title of the book italicized? _____

❸ Look at the questions above again. Put a star * next to each question in which there is a problem. Show this paper to your partner and point to the stars * where he/she needs to improve.

Exercise 18: Write a final draft of your **Source Essay**.

To the Teacher: see the Teacher's Manual for these photocopyable materials:
- Essay with a Source Check-list
- Essay with a Source Evaluation Form

Part 2: *Mixed-Mode Essay*

In this part, first, you will read and analyze a sample essay, in which each paragraph of the body uses a different mode (for example, narration, exposition, argumentation, etc.) Next, you will choose a topic and write a mixed-mode essay.

Strategy 7	Use a different mode in each paragraph of the body of the essay.

Exercise 19

❶ Read the essay, "Thoughts about Life."
❷ From the box below, choose the mode that is used for each part of the essay. Use each mode one time.

Modes

• Comparison and Contrast   ✓ • Exposition   • Argumentation

• Describing a person   • Narration (a story)

Topic: What I can tell the younger generation about life.

	Thoughts about Life
Introduction (No mode) **(Introduction type**: Quotation) *Exposition*	[1] My favorite teacher often told me, "Find a need and fill it." In other words, he was saying that I shouldn't just follow what everyone else was doing. Instead, I should find something that no one else was doing but that people wanted. That became one of my goals in life. I have also learned useful suggestions about life from many other people who were older than me. Here, I would like to share with the younger generation what I have learned about how to have a happy and successful life. [2] It seems that there are three things that are necessary to be happy in life. First, people should have a good family relationship. This does not necessarily mean that they need to have children. It doesn't even mean that they need a spouse. It means that they have someone or several people whom they feel close to. In addition to close relationships, they

should do work that they enjoy. Because people spend so many hours working, if they hate their job, they will dislike a large percent of their life. I spend 50 hours a week doing my job, and I love those 50 hours. Finally, it's important to have something that they enjoy during their free time. It can be a hobby, sports, art or even volunteer work. These three elements can make them feel fulfilled.

[3] The younger generation should not feel regret about past experiences. When I was a teenager in the U.S., I always wanted to live and work in a foreign country. When I was 17 years old, I found a summer job in Canada at a resort. One week before leaving for Canada, my younger brother got very sick, so my parents told me that I had to cancel my plans and stay home to help take care of him. I was very upset and refused to talk to my father during that summer. For 20 years, I thought about that Canadian experience and felt regret about not going. However, last year, I learned that my brother had decided to become a doctor after seeing how much I helped him when he was sick. I now realize that I had only one chance to help my brother, but I still have opportunities to go to Canada. Thus, I wasted 20 years of feeling regret.

[4] People from a younger generation may have a life similar to mine in some ways, but it will surely be different in other ways. Like me, they will have computers to improve their lives. However, their computers will do more work for them, such as preparing their meals and giving them information while driving their car. Likewise, they will have good medicine to help them live longer, just as I have. However, thanks to new medicines, they will suffer less as they get older. For my heart, I have to take medicine which makes me sleepy. Unlike me, when they get older, if they have heart problems, the medicine that they take will probably not have such a side-effect. I hope that they can appreciate these improvements.

⁵ Other people can have a positive effect on younger people if they are able to be aware. When I was growing up, there was a man named Joe, who worked for my father in his clothing store. Joe wasn't very handsome; he was chubby and almost bald. He hated school, so he never graduated from high school. However, he was very artistic. He was a great salesman because he understood colors, and, as a result, he could help customers choose the right clothes. Many of his customers were very important people, for example, presidents of large companies. They had complete trust in his judgments about clothes. He had a talent, and he used it to help many people, namely his customers. I learned from Joe that if we use our talents, we can overcome our weak points.

⁶ Some people believe that success comes from being talented and that a talent is something that comes from our genes. In other words, they claim that a successful person is actually just lucky to have a special talent. However, I disagree with their opinions. We may be born with a tendency to be good at something, but unless we work hard at it, we will never become successful. For example, one of my favorite authors is Barbara Kingsolver. Many people tell her that they admire her because she is so talented. They seem to believe that writing great books is easy for her because she has a special talent. Nevertheless, she claims that her success comes from hard work. She revises every page over and over again; sometimes it will take her six hours to write one good page.

Conclusion (No mode)

(**Conclusion type**: Your experience with the topic.)

⁷ I often felt that I had made many mistakes in my life. Sometimes, I felt that I was a failure. Nevertheless, when I look at the information that I wrote above, I realize that I have learned a lot about life. Perhaps, my life is not a complete success, but I think that I have a philosophy that has helped me over the years.

Essay: *Essay with a Source* • **Part 2:** *Mixed-Mode Essay* • **129**

☛ **First draft assignment**

Exercise 20

❶ Choose one of the topics below.

❷ Write an introduction. (See p. 50 for introduction techniques.)

❸ Write an essay in which you use a different mode for each paragraph in the body. The modes are:

- Description
- Narration
- Exposition
- Compare and contrast
- Cause and Effect
- Extended Definition
- Argumentation
- Process

❹ Write a conclusion. (See p. 53 for conclusion techniques.)

Topics for a Mixed-Mode Essay

- Which one of these characteristics is the most important for a successful life: honesty, courage, friendliness, attractiveness, intelligence, good health, good attitude or good humor?

- What advice would you give to a student from your country who is planning to come to this school and town?

- Are subjects like music and art a waste of time and money for a school to offer?

- Is plagiarism a serious problem? Should students who plagiarize be severely punished?

- Many people believe that there is no such thing as bad luck. They believe, in other words, that misfortune (a hardship) is caused by bad planning or incompetence (such as a lack of skill or stupidity). Do you agree with this opinion?

Strategy 8   Listen to your partner read your essay to you.

Exercise 21

After you finish your second draft:

❶ Exchange essays with a classmate.

❷ Read your classmate's essay silently.

❸ Read your classmate's essay aloud to them.

❹ Your classmate will read your essay aloud to you. You can ask them to stop reading at any time and ask for advice.

Exercise 22

Write a final draft of the **Mixed-Mode Essay**.

To the Teacher: see the Teacher's Manual for these photocopyable materials:
- Mixed-Mode Essay Check-list
- Mixed-Mode Essay Evaluation Form

Section 2: **Fluency Writing**

A Fluency Writing 1

Before Step 1:
1. Silently read the article below.
2. Write answers to the comprehension questions below.

Removing Tattoos (part 1)

Jennifer went out with some friends one evening, got drunk, and got a tattoo. Soon, she realized that she had made a big mistake and now wants to get rid of it. **Do you understand?**

For people like Jennifer, having their tattoos removed will cost a lot of money and cause pain. Removing tattoos by laser is becoming more and more common. Unfortunately, it's expensive and painful. It may also leave a scar and is only 90 percent successful. **Do you want me to explain that again?**

One 30-year-old investment banker wants to have his tattoo removed. Since he is now a member of the business world, he feels embarrassed by his tattoo and does not want his co-workers to know that he has one. **Got it?**

Tom, a construction worker, got his first tattoo when he was 17 years old. That was 10 years ago, and the tattoo is a large snake on his right shoulder. When he first got it, he liked it because, at that time, it was not trendy (in other words, it was not popular) to have one; he liked to be different from other people.

However, now, tattoos have become a fad, so Tom is embarrassed about his tattoo and wants to remove it. It seems that nowadays, a person is unique if he <u>does not</u> have a tattoo. **Understand?**

Step 1:
1. Read your article to your partner. If they don't understand something, try to explain in different words.
2. Ask your partner these comprehension questions.

Comprehension Questions
1. Why did Jennifer get a tattoo?
2. How does Jennifer feel about her tattoo now?
3. Are tattoo removals always completely successful?
4. Why does the investment banker want to get rid of his tattoo?
5. Why did Tom, the construction worker, get a tattoo? Also, why does he want to have it removed?
6. Do you know anyone with a tattoo? What does it look like?

Step 2:
1. Listen to your partner read the second part of the article. If you don't understand something, ask them to explain in different words.

2. Answer their comprehension questions.

Step 3: Do the exercise on page 134.

Fluency Writing 1

DO NOT LOOK AT YOUR PARTNER'S PAGE.

Before Step 1:
1. Silently read the article below.
2. Write answers to the comprehension questions below.

Removing Tattoos (part 2)

This is the second part of the article.

A tattoo that costs only about $30 to have drawn on an arm will cost about $1,500 to be removed by laser. It usually takes several sessions at a doctor's office to remove even a small tattoo completely. Each session lasts about 15 minutes. The next session can happen only after the treatment that was done at the previous session heals, which takes about six weeks. Depending on the size of the tattoo, the full treatment might require six or seven sessions and could take more than a year to complete. Each 15-minute session costs about $300. **Do you understand?**

Tattoo removals by laser are better than older removal systems, but laser is still not perfect. If the tattoo is on the shoulder, there's a high risk of getting a scar. Also, people with darker skin, like African-Americans, have a greater chance of getting a scar. **Got it?** Laser technology works best on removing black and white but not very well on other colors, such as yellow, green, and red.

One doctor recommends that if a young man with a girlfriend wants a tattoo saying "I love Jane," he should get it in black and white, not color, because it will be easier to remove in the future. **Want me to explain that again?**

Step 1:
1. Listen to your partner read the first part of the article. If you don't understand something, ask them to explain in different words.
2. Answer their comprehension questions.

Step 2:
1. Read your article to your partner. If they don't understand something, try to explain in different words.
2. Ask your partner these comprehension questions.

Comprehension Questions

1. How much does it cost to have a tattoo drawn on an arm?
2. How much does it cost to have it removed?
3. How long does each removal session take?
4. Why do we need six weeks between sessions?
5. In what way is laser removal still not perfect?
6. Why did the doctor recommend not getting the words "I love Jane" tattooed in color?
7. This is a discussion question. All of us should answer it. Do you know anyone who has a tattoo? Describe it.

Step 3: Do the exercise on page 134.

Fluency Writing 1

Students

A & B

Step 3: Fluency Writing Exercise

1. Write the information from the article "Removing Tattoos" with as many details as possible. You can use the "Key Words and Phrases" in the box to write your paper.
2. Write about the information from **both parts of the article** (Part 1 and Part 2), not just your part.

Key Words and Phrases

- Jennifer [1*]
- got drunk [2]
- get rid of [3]
- laser [4]

- expensive [5]
- painful [6]
- leave a scar [7]
- only 90% successful [8]

- investment banker [9]
- have his tattoo removed [10]
- embarrassed [11]

- construction worker [12]
- not trendy [13]
- fad [14]
- unique [15]

- $30 [16]
- $1,500 [17]
- to be removed [18]
- session [19]

- 15 minutes [20]
- heals [21]
- 6 weeks [22]
- full treatment [23]

- 6 or 7 sessions [24]
- $300 [25]
- better than [26]
- not perfect [27]

- shoulder [28]
- a scar [29]
- color [30]

---

* The numbers indicate the order in which the words and phrases appear in the article.

Section 2: Fluency Writing

Fluency Writing 2

DO NOT LOOK AT YOUR PARTNERS' PAGES.

Before Step 1:
1. Silently read the article below.
2. Write answers to the comprehension questions below.

Shoplifter (part 1)

When Amy was 15 years old, she stole a pair of earrings from a store. Now, 13 years later, she is addicted to shoplifting. The Christmas holiday season is especially difficult for her because shopping is a big part of the tradition. Her only solution is to avoid stores completely. **Did you understand?**

Amy is now 28 years old and is married and the mother of three children. After shoplifting for 13 years, recently, she was finally arrested for trying to shoplift eight videos from a discount store.

Like Amy, many shoplifters do not steal because they really need something. In fact, many of them are middle-class and upper-middle-class adults who have emotional problems. **Got it?**

It is especially difficult for addicted shoplifters to avoid their habit at Christmas time because it is so easy to do it at that time of the year. This is because it is easy to get lost in the crowd. As a result, it is less likely that store employees will notice them. Also, more merchandise is within easy reach at Christmas time. In fact, police say shoplifting doubles during the holiday season. **Understand?**

Step 1:
1. Read your article to your partners. If they don't understand something, explain in different words.
2. Ask your partners these comprehension questions.

Comprehension Questions

1. How old was Amy when she started shoplifting: 10, 15, or 20 years old?

2. Why does she stay away from stores during the Christmas holiday?

3. Do all shoplifters usually steal because they don't have enough money?

4. Why are the holidays an easy time to shoplift?

5. How much does shoplifting increase during the holidays?

Steps 2 & 3:
1. Listen to your partners read the second and third parts of the article. If you don't understand something, ask them to explain in different words.
2. Answer their comprehension questions.

Step 4: Do the exercise on page 138.

B

Fluency Writing 2

DO NOT LOOK AT YOUR PARTNERS' PAGES.

Before Step 1:
1. Silently read the article below.
2. Write answers to the comprehension questions below.

Shoplifter (part 2)

This is the second part of the article.

Many shoplifters steal things that they don't really need. They do it because they just want to get something free. Most of the shoplifters who get caught actually have the money in their wallets to buy what they stole. They just do it because they are addicted to it. It is almost the same as an addiction to drugs. **Did you understand?**

Part 1 mentioned Amy, the 28-year-old mother, who had been shoplifting since she was 15 years old. She stole everything from clothes to videos. She guesses that the total value was over $30,000.

After she was finally caught, she told the police that, when she shoplifted, she felt really excited because she was so good at it. She was also popular with friends because she would give them expensive gifts that she had stolen. **OK?**

Videos were her favorite items to steal. She has more than 500 now. She stole 97 toy bears, all from the same store in the same year. Each bear was worth $15. One day, she stole a $3,000-computer from a department store by walking in with a baby-stroller. However, if she saw one of her children put a pencil or piece of candy in a coat pocket without paying for it, she made them return it. She always told them that it was wrong to take things that did not belong to them. In this way, she kept her shoplifting a secret, even from her kids. **Got it?**

Step 1: Listen to Student A read the first part of the article. If you don't understand something, ask them to explain in different words. Answer their comprehension questions.

Step 2:
1. Read your article to your partners. If they don't understand something, explain in different words.
2. Ask your partners these comprehension questions.

Comprehension Questions
1. Do many shoplifters actually need the things that they steal?
2. What was the total value of the things Amy stole: $3,000, $13,000, or $30,000?
3. What were the two reasons why Amy liked to shoplift?
4. What are some things that she stole?
5. What did she do if her kids put something in their pockets that they hadn't paid for?

Step 3: Listen to Student C read the third part of the article. If you don't understand something, ask them to explain in different words. Answer their comprehension questions.

Step 4: Do the exercise on page 138.

Fluency Writing 2

DO NOT LOOK AT YOUR PARTNERS' PAGES.

Before Step 1:
1. Silently read the article below.
2. Write answers to the comprehension questions below.

Shoplifter (part 3)

This is the third part of the article.

Amy, the 28-year-old mother, was very good at stealing things from stores. One reason why she was so good at shoplifting was that she had once worked as a manager at a women's clothing store. As a result, she knew where security cameras were located and which people were probably under-cover security guards. **Understand?**

Finally, Amy was caught trying to steal eight videos. When the security guard tried to catch her, she refused to stop and quickly went to her car and drove away. However, the guard got Amy's license plate number, and soon police officers arrived at her home. In the end, Amy's whole family, including her parents and sisters, found out about her addiction. Needless to say, she was extremely ashamed. **Got it?**

Amy had to pay a fine and attend therapy sessions. Also, she has not gone to a mall since her arrest, and she decided not to go Christmas shopping anymore. **OK?**

Steps 1 & 2:
1. Listen to your partners read the first parts of the article. If you don't understand something, ask them to explain in different words.
2. Answer their comprehension questions.

Step 3:
1. Read your article to your partners. If they don't understand something, explain in different words.
2. Ask your partners these comprehension questions.

Comprehension Questions

1. Why was Amy so good at shoplifting?

2. What happened when a security guard caught her stealing some videos?

3. How were the police able to find her home?

4. Why did she feel extremely ashamed?

5. What two things did Amy have to do as punishment for shoplifting?

6. This is a discussion question. All of us should answer it. Is shoplifting a common problem in your country?

Step 4: Do the exercise on page 138.

Fluency Writing 2

Students

A, B, & C

Step 4: Fluency Writing Exercise

1. Write the information from the article "Shoplifter" with as many details as possible. You can use the "Key Words and Phrases" in the box below to write your paper.
2. Write about the information from **all three parts of the article** (Part 1, Part 2, and Part 3), not just your part.

Key Words and Phrases

- Amy [1]
- addicted to [3]
- (was) arrested [5]
- emotional problems [7]
- crowd [9]
- merchandise [11]
- doubles [13]
- money in their wallets [15]
- total value of $30,000 [17]
- videos / toy bears [19]
- children [21]
- manager at a women's clothing store [23]
- security guard [25]
- police officers [27]
- pay a fine / attend therapy sessions [29]
- Christmas shopping [31]

- 15 years old [2]
- avoid [4]
- middle-class and upper-middle-class adults [6]
- Christmas-time [8]
- store employees [10]
- within easy reach [12]
- something free [14]
- an addiction to drugs [16]
- excited / popular [18]
- baby-stroller [20]
- secret [22]
- security cameras [24]
- license plate number [26]
- extremely ashamed [28]
- mall [30]

Fluency Writing 3

DO NOT LOOK AT YOUR PARTNERS' PAGES.

Before Step 1:
1. Silently read the article below.
2. Write answers to the comprehension questions below.

Internet Addiction (part 1)

According to a recent study, about eight percent of Internet users are addicted to it. "Internet addiction" means that you cannot stop using it, you cannot get away from it, and you need it more and more often. **Understand?**

Internet addicts feel depressed, irritable, or angry when they are not at the computer. Some of them flunk out of school, forget to feed their children, or oversleep in the morning because they spent all night online. **OK?**

Researchers did a survey of internet users in order to find out if people were addicted. Here are three examples of the questions that they asked:

1) Did you ever use the Internet to escape from your problems?
2) Did you ever unsuccessfully try to reduce the amount of time that you spent on the internet?
3) Do you often spend time thinking about the internet when you are no longer at your computer? **Got it?**

Step 1:
1. Read your article to your partners. If they don't understand something, explain in different words.
2. Ask your partners these comprehension questions.

Comprehension Questions

1. What percent of internet users are addicted: 8%, 18%, 28%?

2. What are some characteristics of an Internet addict? (In other words, what emotions do they feel when they are not at the computer?)

3. What are some problems caused by the addiction?

4. What are three questions that researchers asked in the survey in order to find out if Internet users were addicted?

Steps 2 & 3:
1. Listen to your partners read the next parts of the article. If you don't understand something, ask them to explain in different words.
2. Answer their comprehension questions.

Step 4: Do the exercise on page 142.

B

Fluency Writing 3

DO NOT LOOK AT YOUR PARTNERS' PAGES.

Before Step 1:
1. Silently read the article below.
2. Write answers to the comprehension questions below.

Internet Addiction (part 2)

This is the second part of the article.

    There are internet users who spend from 14 to 18 hours a day online. They work 10 hours at the computer at their job and then go home and get online there. In some cases, everybody that they know does the same thing, so they feel that it is normal. **Understand?**

    Here are two stories about computer addicts. One 30-year-old man was on-line more than 100 hours a week. He completely ignored his family and friends and stopped only long enough to sleep. **OK?**

    Another man, who was 21 years old, flunked out of college after he stopped going to class. He had disappeared for a week. His family and friends were looking for him, and the campus police finally found him in the university computer lab. He had spent seven days straight on the internet. **Got it?**

Step 1:
    Listen to Student A read the first part of the article. If you don't understand something, ask them to explain in different words. Answer their comprehension questions.

Step 2:
1. Read your article to your partners. If they don't understand something, explain in different words.
2. Ask your partners these comprehension questions.

Comprehension Questions

1. What do some people consider normal? Why do they think it is normal?

2. What did the 30-year-old man do?

3. Who finally found the college student?

4. How many days had the college student spent online?

Step 3:
    Listen to Student C read the last part of the article. If you don't understand something, ask them to explain in different words. Answer their comprehension questions.

Step 4: Do the exercise on page 142.

---

140 • **Assignment 3:** *Internet Addiction*

Fluency Writing 3

DO NOT LOOK AT YOUR PARTNERS' PAGES.

Before Step 1:
1. Silently read the article below.
2. Write answers to the comprehension questions below.

Internet Addiction (part 3)

This is the third part of the article.

Internet addiction is a big danger for three groups of people. The first is young people who are shy, lonely, or depressed and who are uncomfortable in social situations. A second group who can easily become addicted is people who live in the countryside and don't have much contact with other people. A third group is people who have other kinds of addictions, such as smoking, watching too much TV, etc. **OK?**

If users want to avoid internet addiction, experts say that there are some things they can do. For example, they can set a timer when starting a computer session. Also, experts recommend not eating at the computer. If we eat while we are online, the internet will start to interfere with our daily routine. **Do you want me to repeat that?**

Steps 1 & 2:
1. Listen to your partners read the first parts of the article. If you don't understand something, ask them to explain in different words.
2. Answer their comprehension questions.

Step 3:
1. Read your article to your partners. If they don't understand something, explain in different words.
2. Ask your partners these comprehension questions.

Comprehension Questions

1. What three groups of people are in danger of internet addiction?

2. What are two things that internet users should do in order to avoid becoming addicted?

3. Why should users not eat at the computer?

4. This is a discussion question. All of us should answer it. Do you know anyone who seems addicted to the Internet?

Step 4: Do the exercise on page 142.

Fluency Writing 3

Students

A, B, & C

Step 4: Fluency Writing Exercise

1. Write the information from the article "Internet Addiction" with as many details as possible. You can use the "Key Words and Phrases" in the box below to write your paper.
2. Write about the information from **all three parts of the article** (Part 1, Part 2, and Part 3), not just your part.

Key Words and Phrases

- addict / addiction [1]
- cannot stop [3]
- flunk out of [5]
- online [7]
- questions [9]
- try to reduce the amount of time [11]
- from 14 to 18 hours online [13]
- normal [15]
- ignored [17]
- discovered [19]
- seven days straight [21]
- three groups [23]
- countryside [25]
- set a timer [27]
- interfere [29]

- 8% of internet users [2]
- irritable [4]
- oversleep [6]
- did a survey [8]
- escape from problems [10]
- spend time thinking [12]
- job / home [14]
- 30-year-old man [16]
- college student [18]
- campus police [20]
- big danger [22]
- shy [24]
- other addictions [26]
- recommend not eating [28]
- daily routine [30]

Fluency Writing 4

DO NOT LOOK AT YOUR PARTNER'S PAGE.

Vocabulary expression: "GPA" stands for "grade-point average." It is the average of a student's grades in school. A high GPA is better than a low one.

Before Step 1:
1. Silently read the article below.
2. Write answers to the comprehension questions below.

Research about Electronic Devices and Students' Grades (part 1)

Parents and teachers often express concern that young people are spending too much time using electronic devices like smartphones. They are worried that this habit will have a negative effect on their grades in school. This would result in a lower GPA—in other words, a lower grade-point average. **Did you understand what I just read?** As a result, some instructors have made rules against using these phones during class. However, some students have complained about this rule because they say that they want to use these devices to get information online. They claim that they can actually improve their grades by using them. Researchers recently conducted a study to find out how devices like smartphones affect students' grades. **OK?**

Before this recent research, researchers had already done some studies about the effects that smartphones had on young people. One study found a connection between smartphone use and decreased physical activity. **Got it?** Another study reported that these phones may cause a decrease in a student's ability to focus during class. For example, one student said that if he is feeling bored in class, he will start looking at his phone and also go to websites for social media. Another student said that while she is doing her homework, she often takes a break and sends text messages. **Understand?**

Step 1:
1. Read your article to your partners. If they don't understand something, explain in different words.
2. Ask your partners these comprehension questions.

Comprehension Questions
1. Who is worried that smartphones will cause students to have lower GPAs?
2. Why are some students unhappy with the "no smartphones" rule in class?
3. What is the purpose of the research?
4. What effect do smartphones have on physical activity?
5. What did research tell us about smartphones and the ability to focus during class?

Step 2 &3:
1. Listen to your partners read the next parts of the article. If you don't understand something, ask them to explain in different words.
2. Answer their comprehension questions.

Step 3: Do the exercise on page 146.

Fluency Writing 4

DO NOT LOOK AT YOUR PARTNER'S PAGE.

Vocabulary expression: "GPA" stands for "grade-point average." It is the average of a student's grades in school. A high GPA is better than a low one.

Before Step 1:
1. Silently read the article below.
2. Write answers to the comprehension questions below.

Step 1:
Listen to your partner read the first part of the article. If you don't understand something, ask them to explain in different words. Answer their comprehension questions.

Research about Electronic Devices and Students' Grades (part 2)

This is the second part of the article.

In Part 1, the article explained that the purpose of this research was to find out what effect smartphones had on students' GPAs. In an earlier study, researchers found that students who played a lot of video games had lower GPAs. **OK?** According to a study, students in Europe, Asia and America who used web sites for social media had lower GPAs than students who didn't. A common expression nowadays is "multi-tasking." This means doing two or more things at the same time. **Understand?** And, in fact, using a smartphone during a class is a type of multi-tasking. Researchers have, in general, found a negative relationship between multi-tasking and grades. In other words, students who multi-tasked with emails, text messages, and social media had lower scores on tests than students who did not multi-task. **Did you understand what I read?**

As mentioned in the first part of the article, researchers wanted to find out what effect general smartphone use had on grades. However, this is not easy to do. For example, we know from research that, generally speaking, females have higher GPAs than males. So if we find that smartphone users had lower GPAs than non-users, perhaps it was because most of the people in our study were men rather than women. We wouldn't know if the lower GPAs were really connected to smartphones. **Got it?** Similarly, we know that smokers tend to have lower GPAs than non-smokers. Also, students who got high GPAs in high school tended to get higher ones in college. Thus, the researchers had to consider all of these factors. **Did you want me to explain that again?**

Step 2:
1. Read your article to your partners. If they don't understand something, explain in different words.
2. Ask your partners these comprehension questions.

Comprehension Questions
1. Did students who played a lot of video games have higher or lower GPAs?
2. What does "multi-tasking" mean?
3. How do students multi-task?
4. What effect does multi-tasking have on GPAs?
5. Why does the article talk about men, women, smokers, non-smokers and high school GPAs?

Step 3:
Listen to Student C read the last part of the article. If you don't understand something, ask them to explain in different words. Answer their comprehension questions.

Step 4: Do the exercise on page 146.

Fluency Writing 4

Vocabulary expression: "GPA" stands for "grade-point average." It is the average of a student's grades in school. A high GPA is better than a low one.

Before Step 1:
1. Silently read the article below.
2. Write answers to the comprehension questions below.

Research about Electronic Devices and Students' Grades (part 3)

This is the third part of the article.

In Parts 1 and 2, we learned about the types of students who got higher and lower GPAs. In this part, I will explain the results of this recent research. This is what researchers found: If we look at two college students who go to the same university, who are the same sex, who had the same GPAs in high school and who had the same smoking habits, we will find that the student who spent more time using smartphones would have a lower GPA than the student who spent less time on phones. In sum, smartphone use seems to have a negative effect on students' GPAs. **Did you understand that?**

Some students will say that they use their electronic devices for academic purposes, for example, to do research. In fact, studies have found that students who do this get better grades than students who don't. So this is a good use of these devices. **OK?** However, in a study, researchers found that between 80 and 90% of college students reported that they generally use their phones for fun activities, rather than educational ones. **Got it?** And because students almost always have their devices with them in class, in the library and on their desks when they are studying, they are more likely to stop focusing on academic work and start to multi-task by surfing the internet, sending and receiving messages, checking social media and playing video games. **Understand?**

Step 1 & 2:
1. Listen to your partners read the first parts of the article. If you don't understand something, ask them to explain in different words.
2. Answer their comprehension questions.

Step 3:
1. Read your article to your partners. If they don't understand something, explain in different words.
2. Ask your partners these comprehension questions.

Comprehension Questions
1. Researchers looked at students who used their phones more, and less, than others. If we look at the use of smartphones of two women university students, which one will probably have a higher GPA?
2. Let's imagine that there are two college students. One of them uses a smartphone a lot. And the other one uses a smartphone only a little. Which one will probably have a higher college GPA?
3. What percent of college students said that they use their smartphones generally for fun?
4. How do students multi-task with their phones? Explain some examples.
5. This is a discussion question. All of us should answer. Do you think that your smartphone has a negative effect on your ability to study? Explain.

Step 4: Do the exercise on page 146.

Fluency Writing 4

Students

A, B, C

Step 4: Fluency Writing Exercise

1. Write the information from the article "Research about Electronic Devices and Students' Grades" with as many details as you can.
   You can use the "Key Words and Phrases" in the box below to write your paper.
2. Write about the information from **all three parts of the article** (Part 1, Part 2, and Part 3), not just your part.

Key Words and Phrases

- electronic devices [1]
- GPA [3]
- conducted a study to find out [5]
- physical activity [7]
- bored [9]
- video games [11]
- females and males [13]
- high school GPAs [15]
- fun activities [17]
- focusing on academic work [19]

- negative effect [2]
- instructor's rules [4]
- affect students' grades [6]
- ability to focus during class [8]
- takes a break [10]
- multi-tasking [12]
- non-smokers [14]
- 80 to 90% of [16]
- in class, in the library and on their desks [18]
- the results of the study found that [2]

A Fluency Writing 5

DO NOT LOOK AT YOUR PARTNERS' PAGES.

Student

Section 2: Fluency Writing

Before Step 1:
1. Silently read the article below.
2. Write answers to the comprehension questions below.

Genes (part 1)

Genes are something that we have in our bodies that decide many characteristics about us. Experts have known for a long time that our genes determine, for example, our size and the color of our eyes, etc. However, recently researchers have found two other ways that genes affect us. **Do you understand?** Part 1 and Part 2 will explain the first way.

     They found that genes decide our level of happiness. How happy we are is not decided by the events that happen to us. According to researchers, we all have a certain level of happiness that is determined by our genes when we are born. No matter what happens to us, good things or bad things, we will always return to that level. If something bad happens, for example, if we have a fight with someone else, we will probably be in a bad mood for a while. After some time has passed, however, our mood will return to its normal level of happiness. It is exactly the same if something good happens; perhaps we will be in an especially good mood for a while but then return to our normal level. **Got it?**

Step 1:
1. Read your article to your partners. If they don't understand something, explain with different words.
2. Ask your partners these comprehension questions.

Comprehension Questions

1. What information about genes have experts known for a long time?

2. What new information did researchers recently find?

3. When is each person's happiness level decided?

4. Imagine that you have a fight with another person. After some time has passed, what happens to your mood?

Steps 2 & 3:
1. Listen to your partners read the next parts of the article. If you don't understand something, ask them to explain in different words.
2. Answer their comprehension questions.

Step 4: Do the exercise on page 150.

Fluency Writing 5

DO NOT LOOK AT YOUR PARTNERS' PAGES.

Before Step 1:
1. Silently read the article below.
2. Write answers to the comprehension questions below.

Genes (part 2)

This is the second part of the article.

     Researchers went to several countries in order to study the connection between our genes and our happiness level. They found that money has little effect on happiness, and so do education, marriage, and family. Any type of good situation might make a person a little happier, but the change is very small, compared to the effects which our genes have. **OK?**

     Most people will feel bad if they lose a lover. On the other hand, they will feel happy if they get a job promotion. However, these good or bad effects on the mood will disappear after about three months.

     Research shows that even people who win a lot of money in a lottery are no happier one year after winning their big prize than they were before they won it. **Got it?** Researchers also studied people who got terrible back injuries that paralyzed their legs (meaning that they had no feeling in their legs). At first, they were depressed; however, after some time, their mood returned to the natural level of happiness that was determined by their genes. **Do you want me to explain that again?**

Step 1:
Listen to Student A read the first part of the article. If you don't understand something, ask them to explain in different words. Answer their comprehension questions.

Step 2:
1. Read your article to your partners. If they don't understand something, explain with different words.
2. Ask your partners these comprehension questions.

Comprehension Questions
1. Did researchers study happiness in only one country?
2. Which had a greater effect on people's happiness: money, education, or genes?
3. After a good or bad event, how long will it usually take for our happiness level to return to normal?
4. After winning the lottery, are most winners still extremely happy one year later?
5. What does "paralyzed" mean?

Step 3:
Listen to Student C read the last part of the article. If you don't understand something, ask them to explain in different words. Answer their comprehension questions.

Step 4: Do the exercise on page 150.

Fluency Writing 5

DO NOT LOOK AT YOUR PARTNERS' PAGES.

Before Step 1:
1. Silently read the article below.
2. Write answers to the comprehension questions below.

Genes (part 3)

This is the third part of the article.

When researchers studied 1,500 pairs of identical twins, they found another way that genes affect our happiness level. Identical twins are two brothers or two sisters who were born at the same time and originally came from the same egg. The genes of identical twins are 100% the same. The researchers studied the cases of twins who were raised together in the same family and twins who were raised apart in separate families. The study found that it did not matter if they were raised together or separately. Each child continued to have the same level of happiness as their twin brother or sister. **Understand?**

Of course, there were some differences in the lives of some of the twins. They had different education levels, different marriage situations, and different salaries. Sometimes, one twin had graduated from a university while the other twin had never finished 8th grade. Some had high-paying jobs while their twins had low-paying jobs. Nevertheless, in all of their situations, the happiness level of the pair of twins was almost the same, even if their situations were completely different. **OK?**

Steps 1 & 2:
1. Listen to your partners read the first parts of the article. If you don't understand something, ask them to explain in different words.
2. Answer their comprehension questions.

Step 3:
1. Read your article to your partners. If they don't understand something, explain with different words.
2. Ask your partners these comprehension questions.

Comprehension Questions

1. What does the expression "identical twins" mean?
2. How many pairs of identical twins did researchers study?
3. What did researchers find out about twins who were raised together and twins raised separately?
4. What did they learn about twins who had different salaries and education?
5. This is a discussion question. All of us should answer it. Do you think that, in general, you have happy genes or sad genes? Explain.

Step 4: Do the exercise on page 150.

Fluency Writing 5

Students

A, B, & C

Step 4: Fluency Writing Exercise

1. Write the information from the article "Genes" with as many details as possible.
   You can use the "Key Words and Phrases" in the box below to write your paper.
2. Write about the information from **all three parts of the article** (Part 1, Part 2, and Part 3), not just your part.

Key Words and Phrases

- characteristics [1]
- level of happiness [3]
- certain level [5]
- good things or bad things [7]
- mood [9]
- money / education / family [11]
- promotion [13]
- three months [15]
- paralyzed [17]
- mood returned [19]
- 100% the same [21]
- it did not matter [23]
- marriage situation [25]
- graduated from [27]
- pair of twins [29]
- completely different [31]

- researchers [2]
- events [4]
- determine [6]
- in a good / a bad [8]
- normal level [10]
- good situation [12]
- good and bad effects [14]
- win the lottery [16]
- depressed [18]
- identical twins [20]
- raised together / separately [22]
- differences [24]
- salaries [26]
- high-paying / low paying jobs [28]
- even if [30]

A

Fluency Writing 6

DO NOT LOOK AT YOUR PARTNERS' PAGES.

Before Step 1:
1. Silently read the article below.
2. Write answers to the comprehension questions below.

Crows (part 1)

Crows are large, black birds that live in many areas of the world. For about four weeks in June, it is "crow season." During this time, the crows are very aggressive, cawing (in other words, making loud noises) and flying at people to scare them. The reason for their aggressive behavior is that their young ones have just hatched. Sometimes, their babies will jump out of the nest before they can fly. They land on the ground below the nest, so the parents try to scare away anyone who comes near their babies. **Understand?**

Research shows that crows are a lot like humans. They have a territory, in other words, an area that they fight to keep. In addition, they are faithful to their mates. This means that a male and a female bird will stay together for life. **OK?** Also, they are very protective of their babies. In fact, some of the young ones stay near their parents all of their lives. The males and females have an equal relationship. For example, they both help build the nest, sit on the eggs, and feed the young ones. **Got it?**

Step 1:
1. Read your article to your partners. If they don't understand something, explain with different words.
2. Ask your partners these comprehension questions.

Comprehension Questions

1. Can we find crows in many places around the world?

2. What happens during "crow season"?

3. Why are crows aggressive at that time?

4. What are some ways in which crows are similar to people?

Steps 2 & 3:
1. Listen to your partners read the next parts of the article. If you don't understand something, ask them to explain in different words.
2. Answer their comprehension questions.

Step 4: Do the exercise on page 154.

Fluency Writing 6

Before Step 1:
1. Silently read the article below.
2. Write answers to the comprehension questions below.

Crows (part 2)

This is the second part of the article.

Crows are very smart birds. Their brains are larger in proportion to their body size than any other bird. **Understand?** They know how to pick up a clam shell, fly up, and drop it so that it will break open. They are able to mimic dogs and even people. In other words, they can make sounds like a dog or a person. **OK?**

Here are some examples of clever things that crows have done. There was a dog in a yard that was surrounded by a fence with a gate. A crow learned how to open the gate so that the dog would run outside. Then, while the dog was gone, the crow would eat the dog's food. **Did you understand?**

Step 1:

Listen to Student A read the first part of the article. If you don't understand something, ask them to explain in different words. Answer their comprehension questions.

Step 2:
1. Read your article to your partners. If they don't understand something, explain with different words.
2. Ask your partners these comprehension questions.

Comprehension Questions
1. Tell me about the crows' brain size.

2. What can they do with clam shells?

3. What kind of sounds can they make?

4. Explain about the dog in the yard.

Step 3:
1. Listen to Student C read the last part of the article. If you don't understand something, ask them to explain in different words.
2. Answer their comprehension questions.

Step 4: Do the exercise on page 154.

Fluency Writing 6

DO NOT LOOK AT YOUR PARTNERS' PAGES.

Before Step 1:
1. Silently read the article below.
2. Write answers to the comprehension questions below.

Crows (part 3)

This is the third part of the article.

Here is another example that shows that crows are very smart birds. They place nuts on a road and wait for a car to drive over the nuts to crack them open.

Once, some bird hunters built a small shelter in which to hide in order to shoot crows. Three hunters entered the shelter. After a while, two of the hunters left the shelter, but the crows stayed in their hiding place because they knew that one more hunter remained inside the shelter. **Got it?**

This last example of their intelligence involves ice fishermen. Often, these fishermen will cut a hole in the ice and put a fishing line into the water in order to catch some fish. Then they will leave for a few minutes to make another hole somewhere else. While the fishermen are away from their first hole, crows will pull the line out of the water in order to eat the bait. Bait is the food that fishermen use to catch fish. **Do you want me to explain that again?**

Steps 1 & 2:
1. Listen to your partners read the first parts of the article. If you don't understand something, ask them to explain in different words.
2. Answer their comprehension questions.

Step 3:
1. Read your article to your partners. If they don't understand something, explain in different words.
2. Ask your partners these comprehension questions.

Comprehension Questions

1. Why do crows put nuts on the road?

2. Explain what happened with the three hunters.

3. Tell me about the ice fishermen.

4. This is a discussion question. All of us should answer it. Did you find any new or surprising information about crows in this article?

Step 4: Do the exercise on page 154.

Fluency Writing 6

Students

A, B, & C

Step 4: Fluency Writing Exercise

1. Write the information from the article "Crows" with as many details as possible.
   You can use the "Key Words and Phrases" in the box below to write your paper.
2. Write about the information from **all three parts of the article** (Part 1, Part 2, and Part 3), not just your part.

Key Words and Phrases

- crow season [1]
- cawing [3]
- nest [5]
- territory [7]
- mates [9]
- equal relationship [11]
- clam shell [13]
- yard / gate [15]
- nuts on a road [17]
- bird-hunters [19]
- hiding place [21]
- hole [23]
- leave [25]

- aggressive [2]
- hatched [4]
- land on the ground [6]
- faithful [8]
- protective of [10]
- brain / in proportion to [12]
- mimic [14]
- dog's food [16]
- crack them open [18]
- small shelter [20]
- ice fishermen [22]
- fishing line [24]
- bait [26]

Section 2: Fluency Writing

A

Fluency Writing 7

DO NOT LOOK AT YOUR PARTNERS' PAGES.

Before Step 1:
1. Silently read the article below.
2. Write answers to the comprehension questions below.

Organ Donation (part 1)

One afternoon, three cars crashed on a highway near Miami, Florida. In one car was a family who had immigrated from Haiti. The family included 7-year-old Frency Vernet and his mother, father, and two siblings. All of them were injured, but Frency, who was not wearing a seatbelt, suffered terribly from a crushing head wound. **Did you understand?**

An emergency medical team took him by helicopter to a large nearby hospital. Do you understand what a helicopter is? Doctors there agreed that he had serious brain damage and soon declared him braindead. **OK?**

Marla Carroll, a nurse at the hospital, wanted to get permission from Mr. Vernet for an organ donation from his son, Frency. Unfortunately, Mr. Vernet was only semi-conscious from his own injuries, so he was unable to understand the request. Carroll, the nurse, then went to Frency's mother, who was waiting to get an X-ray. **Understand?**

Step 1:
1. Read your article to your partners. If they don't understand something, explain with different words.
2. Ask your partners these comprehension questions.

Comprehension Questions

1. What country did the Vernet family come from?

2. What happened to Frency?

3. What did the doctors decide about Frency's condition?

4. What did the nurse want to get from Mr. Vernet?

5. Why was Mr. Vernet unable to understand the request?

Steps 2 & 3:
1. Listen to your partners read the next parts of the article. If you don't understand something, ask them to explain in different words.
2. Answer their comprehension questions.

Step 4: Do the exercise on page 158.

Fluency Writing 7

E
Student

Before Step 1
1. Silently read the article below.
2. Write answers to the comprehension questions below.

Organ Donation (part 2)

This is the second part of the article.

As it said in Part 1, Marla Carroll, a nurse at a Florida hosptial, went to Mrs. Vernet in order to ask her for permission for an organ donation from her son, Frency, who had been hurt in a terrible accident.

However, because Mrs. Vernet was from Haiti, she did not understand English well. As a result, Carroll asked another nurse to translate the request into French. According to the nurses, Mrs. Vernet said, "Yes, you can donate the organs. I have no problem with that." Doctors immediately took out Frency's organs. **Did you understand?**

A few weeks later, the Vernets learned about the donation when they got a letter from the hospital thanking them for "Frency's gift." Now the Vernets want to sue the hospital because they claim that they never gave permission for the organ donation. Got it? Also, they say that taking organs from a dead body is against their cultural beliefs. "My son can never rest in peace because he doesn't have eyes or a heart," said Mr. Vernet. "In Haiti, we bury the whole body, just as we came into this world." **OK?**

Step 1:

Listen to Student A read the first part of the article. If you don't understand something, ask them to explain in different words. Answer their comprehension questions.

Step 2:

1. Read your article to your partners. If they don't understand something, explain with different words.
2. Ask your partners these comprehension questions.

Comprehension Questions
1. Why did they need a translator for Mrs. Vernet?
2. According to the nurses, what did Mrs. Vernet say?
3. How did the Vernets learn about "Frency's gift"?
4. Why do they want to sue the hospital?
5. What is the cultural belief in Haiti concerning dead bodies and organ donations?

Step 3:

Listen to Student C read the last part of the article. If you don't understand something, ask them to explain in different words. Answer their comprehension questions.

Step 4: Do the exercise on page 158.

Section 2: Fluency Writing

C

Fluency Writing 7

DO NOT LOOK AT YOUR PARTNERS' PAGES.

Before Step 1:
1. Silently read the article below.
2. Write answers to the comprehension questions below.

Organ Donation (part 3)

This is the third part of the article.

Situations like the one described in Part 1 and Part 2 have caused a big discussion over the best procedure for obtaining valuable organs. Nowadays, there is a growing list of sick and injured people who are waiting to receive body parts. As a result, some experts worry that hospitals are using high-pressure techniques to get permission to take out the parts. **Understand?** One professor who specializes in this area feels that it was unreasonable to ask a mother who has just lost a child if it is OK to take her child's body parts. It is even more terrible to ask for her permission if she herself is injured and if she doesn't speak English well. **Got it?**

According to Florida law, a hospital has to get permission with a signature on a form or with a recorded message, for example, on a phone answering machine. However, an administrator at one hospital in Florida said that they get someone's spoken permission in only about 10% to 15% of all organ-donation cases. Do you want me to explain that again?

Steps 1 & 2:
1. Listen to your partners read the first parts of the article. If you don't understand something, ask them to explain in different words.
2. Answer their comprehension questions.

Step 3:
1. Read your article to your partners. If they don't understand something, explain in different words.
2. Ask your partners these comprehension questions.

Comprehension Questions

1. What is the big discussion about?

2. Why might some hospitals use high-pressure techniques to get permission?

3. A professor who specializes in this area explained about a situation in which it is unreasonable to ask for permission. What is the situation?

4. What does Florida's law say is necessary for permission for organ donations?

5. What percent of permissions are just spoken?

6. This is a discussion question. All of us should answer it. Are organ donations common in your country? Would be willing to donate your organs? Explain.

Step 4: Do the exercise on page 158.

Fluency Writing 7

Students

A, B, & C

Step 4: Fluency Writing Exercise

1. Write the information from the article "Organ Donation" with as many details as possible. You can use the "Key Words and Phrases" in the box below to write your paper.
2. Write about the information from **all three parts of the article** (Part 1, Part 2, and Part 3), not just your part.

Key Words and Phrases

- immigrated from Haiti [1]
- injured [3]
- head wound [5]
- brain damage [7]
- Marla Carroll [9]
- organ donation [11]
- request [13]
- did not understand [15]
- took out [17]
- sue the hospital [19]
- rest in peace [21]
- big discussion [23]
- high-pressure techniques [25]
- unreasonable [27]
- signature [29]
- spoken permission [31]

- Frency Vernet [2]
- seatbelt [4]
- helicopter [6]
- brain dead [8]
- permission [10]
- semiconscious [12]
- X-ray [14]
- translate the request [16]
- "Frency's gift" [18]
- cultural beliefs [20]
- whole body [22]
- procedures [24]
- professor [26]
- According to Florida law [28]
- recorded message [30]
- 10% to 15% [32]

A

Fluency Writing 8

DO NOT LOOK AT YOUR PARTNERS' PAGES.

Before Step 1:
1. Silently read the article below.
2. Write answers to the comprehension questions below.

TV and Violence (part 1)

Today, many people are worried about the violence in our society. Every day, we read about people killing and injuring other people. Many people blame TV for this problem. They support their opinion with some research. According to one study, a typical 18-year-old person has seen 200,000 acts of violence and 40,000 murders on TV programs. **Do you understand?** People who blame TV for violence also often mention John Hinckley. In 1981, John Hinckley shot President Reagan. Before doing this, Hinckley had spent many hours alone in a room watching TV. Some people believe that Hinckley shot Reagan because TV caused him to confuse fantasy with reality. **Got it?**

Step 1:
1. Read your article to your partners. If they don't understand something, explain with different words.
2. Ask your partners these comprehension questions.

Comprehension Questions

1. What are many people worried about today?

2. How old are the people who have seen 40,000 murders on TV?

3. What did John Hinckley do?

4. What do some people believe caused Hinckley to do this?

Steps 2 & 3:
1. Listen to your partners read the next parts of the article. If you don't understand something, ask them to explain in different words.
2. Answer their comprehension questions.

Step 4: Do the exercise on page 162.

Fluency Writing 8

DO NOT LOOK AT YOUR PARTNERS' PAGES.

Before Step 1:
1. Silently read the article below.
2. Write answers to the comprehension questions below.

TV and Violence (part 2)

This is the second part of the article.

A big question that people ask each other today is: does TV really cause people to become violent? Some people feel that there is little proof of this. One writer for the New York Times made the following comment. Young Americans have seen thousands of murders on TV. However, they have also seen even more acts of kindness. In other words, they have seen TV characters fall in love and help each other. **Understand?** Therefore, he says that we should conclude that TV encourages people to be nice to each other more than it encourages violence. **OK?**

On the other hand, people who believe that TV does cause violence point to a study of children. The study found that children who watched a lot of violent TV programs were violent when they became adults. **Got it?**

Step 1:
Listen to Student A read the first part of the article. If you don't understand something, ask them to explain in different words. Answer their comprehension questions.

Step 2:
1. Read your article to your partners. If they don't understand something, explain with different words.
2. Ask your partners these comprehension questions.

Comprehension Questions

1. What big question do people ask each other today?

2. A writer for the *New York Times* agrees that people see violence on TV. But he also says that they see <u>more of</u> something else. What do they see more of?

3. According to the *New York Times* writer, if TV encourages people to be violent, it should also encourage them to do what?

4. On the other hand, what did the study of the children find?

Step 3:
Listen to Student C read the last part of the article. If you don't understand something, ask them to explain in different words. Answer their comprehension questions.

Step 4: Do the exercise on page 162.

Fluency Writing 8

DO NOT LOOK AT YOUR PARTNERS' PAGES.

Before Step 1:
1. Silently read the article below.
2. Write answers to the comprehension questions below.

TV and Violence (part 3)

This is the third part of the article.

Part 2 described a study that showed that children who watched a lot of violent TV programs were violent when they became adults. However, some experts say that this does not prove that there is a connection between TV and violence. They say that children and adults who <u>already</u> have a violent nature tend to watch more violent TV shows. In other words, some people are naturally violent. It is part of their personality. **Did you understand what I said?** Because of their violent personality, they like to watch violent TV programs. Perhaps John Hinckley, who shot President Reagan, was this kind of person. **OK?**

People who believe that TV does <u>not</u> cause violence like to talk about another study. There is a city in the U.S., called Detroit, which is near a Canadian city, called Windsor. People in <u>both</u> cities watch the same TV shows. However, the murder rate in Detroit is 30 times higher than the murder rate in Windsor. Obviously, TV did not encourage the violence in Detroit. Something else seems to be causing the difference between Detroit and Windsor. **Got it?**

Steps 1 & 2:
1. Listen to your partners read the first parts of the article. If you don't understand something, ask them to explain in different words.
2. Answer their comprehension questions.

Step 3:
1. Read your article to your partners. If they don't understand something, explain in different words.
2. Ask your partners these comprehension questions.

Comprehension Questions

1. What do some experts say about the connection between violence, personality, and TV?

2. The article said, "Perhaps John Hinckley was <u>that kind of person</u>." What does this mean?

3. Tell me about the study of Detroit and Windsor.

5. This is a discussion question. All of us should answer it. Do you think that TV programs or movies or video games cause people to become more violent?

Step 4: Do the exercise on page 162.

Fluency Writing 8

Students

A, B, & C

Step 4: Fluency Writing Exercise

1. Write the information from the article "TV and Violence" with as many details as possible. You can use the "Key Words and Phrases" in the box below to write your paper.
2. Write about the information from **all three parts of the article** (Part 1, Part 2, and Part 3), not just your part.

Key Words and Phrases

- worried about [1]
- research [3]
- 200,000 acts of violence [5]
- John Hinckley [7]
- confuse [9]
- reality [11]
- question [13]
- acts of kindness [15]
- to be nice [17]
- children [19]
- connection between TV and violence [21]
- personality [23]
- Windsor (in Canada) [25]
- 30 times higher [27]
- something else [29]

- blame TV [2]
- typical [4]
- 40,000 murders [6]
- President Reagan [8]
- fantasy [10]
- proof [12]
- writer for the *New York Times* [14]
- encourages people [16]
- study [18]
- violent when they became adults [20]
- violent nature [22]
- Detroit (in the U.S.) [24]
- murder rate [26]
- did not encourage [28]

Section 3: **Grammar**

Individual Work: Units 1, 2, 3, 5, 6, 7, 8, 9, 10, 13, 14, 15, 17, 18, 19, 20, 21, 23, 25, 26, 27

Group Work: Units 4, 12, 16, 22, 24

Grammar Unit 1

Common mistakes: Comma Splices (CS), Run-ons (RO), and Fragments (frag)

Type of mistake	Examples
CS → comma splice	I like music, she likes sports.
RO → run on	I like music she likes sports.
frag → fragment	While she watches sports.

Exercise 1

In the blanks, write . . .
- **OK** if the sentences are grammatically correct.
- **CS** if there is a comma splice.
- **RO** if there is a run-on.
- **frag** if there is a fragment.

_____ 1. He has a strange habit, he often rubs his ear for about 10 seconds.

_____ 2. He has a strange habit. He often rubs his ear for about 10 seconds.

_____ 3. He has a strange habit. He often rubs his ear. For about 10 seconds.

_____ 4. He has a strange habit he often rubs his ear for about 10 seconds.

_____ 5. During an interview, we should have good eye contact with the interviewer because it makes a good impression.

_____ 6. During an interview, we should have good eye contact. Because the interviewer will think that we are friendly.

_____ 7. During an interview, we should have good eye contact. This is because the interviewer will think that we are friendly.

_____ 8. During an interview, we should have good eye contact the interviewer will think that we are friendly.

_____ 9. During an interview, we should have good eye contact, the interviewer will think that we are friendly.

_____ 10. People can accomplish anything if they are motivated. Even if it seems impossible.

_____ 11. People can accomplish anything, they should never give up.

_____ 12. People can accomplish anything they should never give up.

_____ 13. People can accomplish anything, so they should never give up.

Exercise 2

❶ Write **CS** if it is a comma splice, **RO** if it is a run-on sentence, or **frag** if it is a fragment.
❷ Write the sentence correctly.

_____ 1. Our team won the championship we celebrated all night.

Revised: _____

_____ 2. We cancelled our plans for the picnic. Because the weather was rainy.

Revised: _____

_____ 3. People tend to spend more money when they are hungry, we should eat before we

go shopping.

Revised: _____

_____ 4. If you copy from an Internet site for an essay, it's called plagiarism. Some students

do it. Although, it's illegal.

Revised: _____

_____ 5. Since I became a vegetarian, my health has improved I've got more energy too.

Revised: _____

Exercise 3

Write a sentence that has a comma splice (**CS**).

_____

_____

Exercise 4

Write a sentence that has a run-on (**RO**).

_____

_____

Exercise 5

Write a sentence that has a fragment (frag).

_____

_____

Subjects and Verbs

Individual Work

Grammar Unit 2

Section 3: Grammar

$$\boxed{\textbf{S} = \text{subject} \quad \textbf{V} = \text{verb} \quad \textbf{AV} = \text{auxiliary verb}\,_{\text{(helping verb)}}}$$

Examples:

-     ^S   ^V
Sam walked to the park.

- ^S   ^S   ^V
Ann and Tom are students in my class.

-             ^S   ^{AV}   ^V
After visiting China, the travelers could speak Chinese better than before.

- ^S   ^{AV}   ^V   ^S   ^{AV}   ^V
Larry will study for a year, and then he will look for a job.

- ^S   ^V
I want to ask him this question.
(**Note**: *"to ask"* is <u>not</u> *the verb of the sentence. It is an infinitive.*)

-         ^S   ^{AV}   ^V
Most children are entertained by cartoons.

Exercise 1

❶ Write **S** above the subjects.
❷ Write **V** above the verbs.
❸ Write **AV** above the auxiliary verbs if there are any.

1. Tigers are beautiful animals.

2. We want to go to the basement, if possible.

3. Tony and Karen were cheating on the test and were caught by the teacher.

4. They needed to find the key to the door.

5. I am in Computer Science, and he is in Math.

6. Most tourists will have some problems finding hotels.

7. These flowers were given to me by my neighbor.

Exercise 2

Use the patterns to write sentences.

❶ Write **S** above the subjects.
❷ Write **V** above the verbs.
❸ Write **AV** above the auxiliary verbs (if there are any).

            S   S V
Example: S-S-V : Mary and Tom ate lunch together.

1. S-AV-V :

2. S-V-V :

3. S-V-S-V :

4. S-S-AV-V-AV-V :

Grammar Unit 3
Conjunctions

S	V	, CONJ	S	V
		(conjunction)		
		, and		
		, but		
		, so		
		, or		

Examples:

-      S V   CONJ S AV V

  We had dinner, but we didn't go to a movie.

-            S   V   CONJ   S   V

  My older sister works as a receptionist, and my younger brother drives a bus.

Exercise 1

❶ Write **S** above the subjects.
❷ Write **V** above the verbs.
❸ Write **AV** above the auxiliary verbs (if there are any).
❹ Write **CONJ** above the conjunctions.

1. They invited us to their home, so we could see their new baby.

2. Will you take me to the airport tomorrow, or should I call for a taxi?

3. Tom had planned on visiting Africa, but he lost his passport.

4. My math teacher wants me to finish my homework, and my history teacher has asked me to stay after class.

Exercise 2

❶ Write four sentences using a conjunction (**and, but, so, or**) in each sentence.
❷ Write **S** above the subjects.
❸ Write **V** above the verbs.
❹ Write **AV** above the auxiliary verbs if there are any.
❺ Write **CONJ** above the conjunctions.

About Group Work

Units 4, 12, 16, 18, 22, and 24 have been designed for Group Work. In group work, you will have a page marked "Student A, B, or C." On your page, you will find a worksheet and directions explaining what to do with it.

This is very important:

DO NOT LOOK AT YOUR PARTNERS' PAGES.

A

Grammar Unit 4

Prepositional Phrases

Directions

Read these directions and questions about the worksheet below to your partners.

1. Look at Sentences A and B. Circle the prepositions.

4. Look at Sentence F. Do we need to add a preposition?

7. Look at Sentence H. Underline the two prepositional phrases.

10. Look at Exercise 3. Read the information about prepositional phrases. Do you understand it?

13. Look at Sentence M. Underline the prepositional phrase. Then write "S" above the subject.

16. Look at Sentence P. Should we put "has" or "have" in the blank? Why?

Worksheet

Exercise 1

A. His house is by the river.

B. The presents were under a blanket in the closet.

C. The electricity i____ our house went out du_____ the storm.

D. At Friday evenings, we usually go to a movie.

E. She told to me that I was chosen.

F. After Tom finished work, he went shopping.

Exercise 2: a prepositional phrase = a preposition + noun phrase or pronoun

   Example: The dog barked <u>at the stranger</u>.
   (*"at the stranger" is a prepositional phrase: **at** is a preposition; **the stranger** is a noun phrase.*)

G. We spent the afternoon at the beach.

H. He fell on his bed, put a pillow over his face, and tried to sleep.

I. She left early because she was feeling a pain in _____

J. _____, Sam has a dentist appointment.

Exercise 3: Note: *prepositional phrases **cannot** be subjects of sentences.*

K. The man near the door is my father.

L. During the lecture, the instructor wrote on the board.

M. The water in the bathtub was very hot.

N. Tonight, the programs on TV _____ not very interesting.

O. Toward the end of my vacation, I received a letter about my new job.

P. The man with the three dogs _____ a sports car.

Q. In the morning is hard to wake up.

Prepositional Phrases • Directions

Read these directions and questions about the worksheet below to your partners.

2. Look at Sentence C. Fill in the prepositions.

5. Look at Exercise 2. Read the information about a prepositional phrase. Do you understand it?

8. Look at Sentence I. Circle the preposition and complete the prepositional phrase.

11. Look at Sentence K. Write "S" above the subject.

14. Look at Sentence N. Should we put "is" or "are" in the blank? Why?

17. In Sentence Q, what is the problem?

Worksheet

Exercise 1

A. His house is by the river.

B. The presents were under a blanket in the closet.

C. The electricity i____ our house went out du_____ the storm.

D. At Friday evenings, we usually go to a movie.

E. She told to me that I was chosen.

F. After Tom finished work, he went shopping.

Exercise 2: a prepositional phrase = a preposition + noun phrase or pronoun

Example: The dog barked <u>at the stranger</u>.
(*"at the stranger" is a prepositional phrase:* **at** *is a preposition;* **the stranger** *is a noun phrase.*)

G. We spent the afternoon at the beach.

H. He fell on his bed, put a pillow over his face, and tried to sleep.

I. She left early because she was feeling a pain in _____

J. _____, Sam has a dentist appointment.

Exercise 3: Note: *prepositional phrases* **cannot** *be subjects of sentences.*

K. The man near the door is my father.

L. During the lecture, the instructor wrote on the board.

M. The water in the bathtub was very hot.

N. Tonight, the programs on TV _____ not very interesting.

O. Toward the end of my vacation, I received a letter about my new job.

P. The man with the three dogs _____ a sports car.

Q. In the morning is hard to wake up.

Prepositional Phrases • Directions

Read these directions and questions about the worksheet below to your partners.

3. Look at Sentences D and E. Are there any mistakes with the prepositions? Explain.

6. Look at Sentence G. What is the noun phrase after the preposition?

9. Look at Sentence J. Write a prepositional phrase in the blank.

12. Look at Sentence L. Is the word "lecture" the subject of the sentence? How do you know?

15. Look at Sentence O. Underline the prepositional phrases. Then write "S" above the subject of the sentence.

18. On page 173, let's do Exercise 1 together.

Worksheet

Exercise 1

A. His house is by the river.

B. The presents were under a blanket in the closet.

C. The electricity i____ our house went out du_____ the storm.

D. At Friday evenings, we usually go to a movie.

E. She told to me that I was chosen.

F. After Tom finished work, he went shopping.

Exercise 2: a prepositional phrase = a preposition + noun phrase or pronoun

Example: The dog barked at the stranger.
*("at the stranger" is a prepositional phrase: **at** is a preposition; **the stranger** is a noun phrase.)*

G. We spent the afternoon at the beach.

H. He fell on his bed, put a pillow over his face, and tried to sleep.

I. She left early because she was feeling a pain in _____

J. _____, Sam has a dentist appointment.

Exercise 3: Note: *prepositional phrases **cannot** be subjects of sentences.*

K. The man near the door is my father.

L. During the lecture, the instructor wrote on the board.

M. The water in the bathtub was very hot.

N. Tonight, the programs on TV _____ not very interesting.

O. Toward the end of my vacation, I received a letter about my new job.

P. The man with the three dogs _____ a sports car.

Q. In the morning is hard to wake up.

Grammar Unit 5
Prepositions

Exercise 1: Draw a line through the words that **are not prepositions.** *Remember:* Prepositions are followed by a noun or noun phrase. **Note:** <u>Ten</u> *of these words are not prepositions.*

above	become	from	often	through
according to	below	frequently	on	to
~~also~~	beside	in	outside	toward
among	between	inside	over	under
around	by	just	soon	while
at	during	near	set	with
be	for	of	then	
because of				

Exercise 2

❶ <u>Underline</u> the prepositional phrases if there are any.

❷ Write "S" above the subjects of the sentences.

1. With great effort, Sam was able to finish the job.
2. He left for work at 6 a.m. on the bus.
3. My friend taught me how to make spaghetti.

Exercise 3: Fill in the blanks with prepositions.

1. _____ April, we will have a week off.
2. _____ April 15, they'll leave for Europe.
3. We rode on the train _____ three hours.
4. It must have rained _____ the night.

Exercise 4: Fill in the blanks with **During** or **While.**

1. _____ the movie, we ate popcorn.
2. _____ we were watching the movie, we ate popcorn.
3. _____ is a preposition. It is followed by a noun phrase or pronoun.
4. _____ is **not** a preposition. It is followed by a noun and verb.
5. Write a sentence with "During." _____

   _____

6. Write a sentence with "While." _____

   _____

Exercise 5

   ❶ ⬭Circle⬭ the prepositions.

   ❷ Complete the sentences.

1. They stopped at _____

2. During _____, my brother became sick.

3. Inside _____, the old man talked to _____

   about _____

4. According to _____

_____

Exercise 6

   ❶ Write **S** above the subjects.

   ❷ Write **V** above the verbs.

   ❸ ⬭Circle⬭ the prepositions.

1. After the trip, they unpacked their suitcases.

2. Because of the storm warnings, everyone went home early.

3. The leaders of that country asked the citizens with extra food to share it with their neighbors.

Exercise 7: Choose five prepositions from Exercise 1 on page 173 and write a sentence with each.

   ❶ Write **S** above the subjects.

   ❷ Write **V** above the verbs.

   ❸ ⬭Circle⬭ the prepositions.

_____

_____

_____

_____

_____

_____

_____

_____

_____

_____

Grammar Unit 6
Independent and Dependent Clauses

Clause: a group of words that contains a <u>subject</u> and <u>verb</u>

Exercise 1

Write **clause** next to each clause.

_____ 1. Chicago is a city

_____ 2. in a restaurant

_____ 3. before 5 p.m.

_____ 4. before they got sick

_____ 5. during that awful movie

_____ 6. which I need to buy

Independent clause (e.g., "We always spend our vacations there")
Dependent clause (e.g., "If I had a problem")

Exercise 2: Choose the right answer.

1. An independent clause _____ be a sentence by itself.
                            (can or cannot)

2. A dependent clause _____ be a sentence by itself.
                          (can or cannot)

Exercise 3

❶ Write **Independent** next to the independent clauses.
❷ Write **Dependent** next to the dependent clauses.

_____ 1. he was a great man

_____ 2. the newspaper was late today

_____ 3. after we left for work

_____ 4. the child's toy broke

_____ 5. because my car is dirty

_____ 6. where my sister went to school

_____ 7. although it didn't snow very much

_____ 8. people tend to catch colds in the winter

_____ 9. why seat belts are required

_____10. when he practices a lot

Grammar Unit 6: *Independent and Dependent Clauses* • **175**

Grammar Unit 7
Subordinators

> **Subordinators** are followed by clauses: *while I was writing*
>
> The subordinator and its clause are a **dependent clause**: *She talked while I was writing*.
>
> Some subordinators: *because, if, when, while, as soon as, before, even if, although, until, even though*

Exercise 1

❶ Circle the subordinators.

❷ Underline the dependent clauses.

1. We couldn't drive any further (because) we were out of gas.
2. While the sun was setting, they ate dinner on the boat.
3. The fire truck came as soon as it received the call.
4. When you feel hungry, you should eat some fruit.
5. You will not get better if you refuse to see a doctor.

   (*Remember: **to see** is **not** the verb of the clause; it is an infinitive.*)

6. Frank tries to use public transportation even though he owns a car.
7. Before Ann bought her dog, she had only a pet cat.
8. During the trip, we drove until it became dark.
9. As soon as we find the instructions, we can start the game.
10. I plan to stay in this apartment until my landlord raises the rent.

Exercise 2

❶ Circle the subordinators.
❷ Underline the dependent clauses.
❸ For the *independent clauses*, write **S** and **V** above the subjects and verbs, and **AV** above the auxiliary verbs (if there are any).
❹ For the *dependent clauses*, write **S** and **V** above the subjects and verbs, and **AV** above the auxiliary verbs (if there are any).

1. (After) he had found the mistake, he corrected it.
2. She will appear on TV as soon as she finishes her book.
3. Even if he loses the election, he plans to celebrate.

   (*Remember: **to celebrate** is **not** the verb of the clause.*)

4. My mother had forgotten to remove the price tag from the gift before she wrapped it.

5. My computer has caused a lot of problems even though it was very expensive.

6. Because his car wouldn't start, Ken missed the meeting.

7. I like to read magazines while I wait for the bus to arrive.

Exercise 3: Circle the subordinators and underline the dependent clauses.

1. Although it upsets her stomach, Sue drinks a lot of coffee while she reads the morning newspaper.

2. When the concert was over, everyone began to clap because the performance had been very enjoyable.

3. After the snow stopped falling, they drove to the mountain and skied for 4 hours.

4. Fortunately, the police were able to find the lost boy before night came, but they couldn't tell us if he was hurt.

5. Even though Tom was able to save a lot of money from his job, he still doesn't have enough to travel to Europe with us since we plan to stay for at least a month.

Exercise 4: This exercise will prepare you for Exercise 6.

Sentences with advanced ideas do not have mistakes and are about topics that you haven't often written about. Also, some of them will have a conjunction or more than one subordinator. Examples of *advanced* topics:

- current news
- ideas from books
- ideas from your academic courses
- ideas from movies
- problems that people have
- unique people that you know

Sentences with simple sentences are about topics that people commonly write about. Examples of simple topics:

- your daily life
- your classroom
- your bedroom
- your free time

Directions

❶ Write **A** in the blank if the idea is advanced.

❷ Write **S** in the blank if the idea is simple.

__ 1. **Because** many people were suffering in a number of foreign countries, the Red Cross was sending aid to them.

__ 2. **Because** I'm tired, I will go to sleep.

__ 3. I will work at my computer **until** I finish my homework.

__ 4. Women will not earn as much money as men **until** they are given positions as managers in companies.

__ 5. **As soon as** snow starts to fall, drivers should slow down **because** it is difficult to stop suddenly on wet roads.

__ 6. **As soon as** I get up in the morning, I check my phone messages.

__ 7. I read an article that said that **if** we are kidnapped, we should not try to escape **unless** we know where we can run to.

__ 8. **If** you feel sick, you should go to a doctor.

Exercise 5: Look at the *advanced* sentences in Exercise 4 above again.

• What are the numbers of the two sentences that had more than one subordinator? __ and __

Exercise 6

❶ Write six sentences with a dependent and independent clause. Use the subordinators below. Try to write some advanced sentences with more than one subordinator and dependent clause.
❷ (Circle) the subordinators.
❸ Underline the dependent clauses.
❹ You should write six *advanced* sentences.

Examples:

1. **if**: (If) he gets sick, he should see a doctor.

2. **whenever**: (Whenever) Tom's alarm clock rings early in the morning, his roomate turns it off.

Subordinators

• before	• because	• unless
• while	• whenever	• until
• although	• if	• when
• after	• even though	• as soon as

Grammar Unit 8
Noun Clauses

Noun Clause: a kind of dependent clause

"That" can introduce a dependent clause. *I know that you are my friend.*
"That" can be omitted. *I know you are my friend.*

Incorrect: He **doubts me to be** able to finish the project.
Correct: He **doubts** <u>that I will be able to finish the project.</u>
(noun clause)

Incorrect: Their friends **suggested** them to make a reservation.
Correct: Their friends **suggested** <u>that they make a reservation.</u>
(noun clause)

Verbs which are commonly followed by **that** + noun clause:

- believe
- realize
- suggest
- forget
- say
- wonder
- hope
- worry
- recommend
- know
- remember
- understand
- think
- doubt

Exercise 1

❶ (Circle) the subordinator.
❷ <u>Underline</u> the noun (dependent) clauses.
❸ Write **V** above the verb of the independent clause.

1. I know (that) my parents were there.

2. The passengers worried that their plane would arrive late.

3. The actor realized that he didn't know his lines.

4. The pilot hoped that he could fly to some foreign countries.

5. The doctor thought that he could help the patient.

6. He always says that he can do it.

7. Tom believed that that was the problem.

8. Kathy forgot that she had to go to a meeting.

9. I understand that we need a ticket.

> Question words *(who, what, when, where, why, how)* can also be subordinators:
> *I know who he is.*
>
> But notice that the word order of the question can change:
> *Who is he? > I know who he is.*

Exercise 2

❶ (Circle) the subordinator.
❷ Underline the (noun) dependent clauses.
❸ Write **V** above the verb of the independent clause.

1. I don't know how my parents discovered my secret.

2. She realized why she had failed the test.

3. Nobody believed what the child said.

4. We wonder why he did that.

5. I forgot how I did it.

6. My boss suggested how I could improve my work.

7. He remembered when his appointment was.

8. I don't understand why she wants to leave now.

In the sentences above, which verbs introduced the noun clauses?

1. _____   2. _____   3. _____   4. _____
5. _____   6. _____   7. _____   8. _____

Exercise 3

Write <u>four sentences</u> with noun clauses.

❶ (Use verbs) that are commonly followed by noun clauses.
❷ Use subordinators that commonly introduce noun clauses.
❸ Circle the subordinator.
❹ Underline the noun clause

Example: Sue believed <u>that someone had secretly listened to her phone conversations</u>.

Grammar Unit 9
Reduced Adverb Clauses

Commonly used subordinators

After / Before / While / Since

Examples

1. *While I was __walking__ to class, I ran into an old friend.*
   a. Underline the adverb (dependent) clause.
      • *While I was __walking__ to class, I ran into an old friend.*
   b. Reduce the adverb clause to a modifying phrase (take out the subject and *be* verb).
      • *While __walking__ to class, I ran into an old friend.*

2. *After I __had eaten__ breakfast, I left for work.*
   a. Underline the adverb (dependent) clause.
      • *After I __had eaten__ breakfast, I left for work.*
   b. Reduce the adverb clause to a modifying phrase (take out the subject and change the verb to -*ing*):
      • *After __eating__ breakfast, I left for work.*

Exercise 1

❶ Underline the adverb (dependent) clause.
❷ Reduce the adverb clause to a modifying phrase:

1. Since he bought a computer, he has been able to work faster.

   _____

2. After I had finished my work, I went to the movies.

   _____

3. She broke her leg while she was playing soccer.

   She broke her leg while _____

4. You should study hard before you take a test.

   _____

Exercise 2

❶ Circle the subjects of the dependent and independent clauses.

❷ Underline the adverb (dependent) clause.

❸ Reduce the adverb clause to a modifying phrase.

1. Since we came here, we've learned a lot of English.

   _____

2. I found the keys after I searched through my desk drawers.

   _____

Exercise 3

❶ Circle the subjects of the dependent and independent clauses.

❷ Underline the adverb (dependent) clause.

   • While I was driving the car, the baby fell asleep.

Question A: In the sentence above, can we reduce the adverb clause to a modifying phrase? (e.g. a phrase like *While driving the car, the baby fell asleep.*) _____

Question B: If we want to reduce to an adverb phrase, what must be the same in the dependent and independent clauses? _____

Exercise 4

If possible, reduce the clauses to phrases.

1. After the police had stopped the fight, they arrested two men.

2. I had shut off the lights before I left the room.

3. Before Steve had returned to his country, his roommate threw a farewell party for him.

4. Since they left home, they have felt homesick.

5. Tom got a flat tire while he was driving to work.

6. Ken talked to his girlfriend on the phone while his mother was cooking dinner.

7. After the pilot had landed the plane, the flight attendant said, "Goodbye" to the passengers.

Exercise 5

Complete the sentences with the correct form of the verb.

1. Before (leave) _____ on his trip, Bill got a passport.

2. Before he (leave) _____ on his trip, Bill had gotten a passport.

3. She has become more self-confident since she (learn) _____ how to play the piano.

4. She has become more self-confident since (learn) _____ how to play the piano.

5. After (take) _____ this medicine, you shouldn't drive a car.

6. Because he (take) _____ the medicine, I drove the car.

7. I took the wrong turn while I (drive) _____to my uncle's house.

8. While (drive) _____ on the wrong road, I almost hit a moose.

9. After the special guest (arrive) _____, the party will begin.

10. After (arrive) _____ at the party, the guest gave an interesting talk about her trip to China.

Exercise 6

Editing: *If possible*, change the underlined clauses to phrases.

There are some steps that airline passengers can take to prevent jet lag. First, before <u>they start</u> their trip, they should drink plenty of water. Also, just before <u>they leave</u>, they should eat a meal with protein and carbohydrates. Next, during the flight, they should avoid all medications or sleeping pills. While <u>they are sitting</u> in the plane, they should do some stretching exercises. Before <u>the flight attendants serve</u> dinner, the passengers should walk around occasionally. Finally, after <u>the bus or taxi drops</u> them off at their hotel, the travelers should take a short nap.

Grammar Unit 10

Restrictive and Non-Restrictive Clauses

Restrictive Clauses . . .	Non-Restrictive Clauses . . .

give new (NECESSARY) information.
 • do not use commas
 • begin with *that, which, who*
 • do <u>not</u> come after proper nouns
   (e.g. Mr. Jones, Seattle)
	give extra (UNNECESSARY) information.
	 • use commas
	 • begin with *which, who* (but <u>not</u> ***that***)
	 • can come after proper nouns
	   (e.g. Professor Smith, Disneyland)

1. My sister attends a university *which is very well-known.* 2. Babies *who are born with black hair* sometimes grow blond hair later. 3. Rice *that is grown in the U.S.* is drier than rice *that is grown in Asia.*	1. My sister attends Harvard University, *which is very well-known.* 2. Babies, *who can't speak when they are born,* develop language skills over the next few years. 3. Rice, *which is an important crop in Asia ,* is used in some European and Latin American dishes.

Exercise 1

❶ (Circle) the subordinators (***who, which, that***).
❷ <u>Underline</u> the dependent clauses.

1. People (who) work on holidays can make extra money.

2. Next January, we plan to visit Hawaii, which is warm even in winter.

3. The Internet, which is available almost everywhere, is an important source of information.

4. Ken is planning to take a French course which includes both speaking and writing.

5. He spent the afternoon at a lecture that lasted four hours, so he is tired now.

6. After talking to Mrs. Wilson, who is my advisor, I decided to change my schedule.

Exercise 2

    ❶ Answer the questions after each sentence.
    ❷ Put in **commas** in the sentences with <u>extra information</u>.

1. Crime in New York <u>which is the nation's largest city</u> has dropped recently.

   Questions: If we did not include the <u>underlined</u> words, would you still know where the crime has dropped? _____ Are these words necessary or extra information? _____

2. In my city, crime <u>which is committed by teenagers</u> has risen recently.

   Questions: If we did not include the <u>underlined</u> words, would you still know what kind of crime has risen? _____ Are these words necessary or extra information? _____

3. Doctors <u>who specialize in sports medicine</u> help teams prepare for games.

   Questions: If we did not include the <u>underlined</u> words, would you still know what kind of doctors will help teams? _____ Are these words necessary or extra information? _____

4. Bill's father <u>who is a marathon runner</u> will help him train for the big race.

   Questions: If we did not include the <u>underlined</u> words, would you still know whose father will help Bill? _____ Are these words necessary or extra information? _____

5. My house <u>which has a basement</u> often gets flooded in the spring.

   Questions: If we did not include the <u>underlined</u> words, would you still know whose house gets flooded? _____ Are these words necessary or extra information? _____

Exercise 3

    ❶ Fill in the blanks with **that**, **which**, or **who.**
    ❷ Put in <u>11 commas</u> (where necessary).

1. New Zealand _____ is an English-speaking country is famous for its beautiful countryside.

2. Apples _____ are green are often not very sweet.

3. Apples _____ are red are usually sweet.

4. My uncle works for Mercedes Benz _____ is a famous car company.

5. We went on a picnic with two groups of children. The children _____ were under 13 years old played soccer, and the ones _____ were over 13 played baseball.

6. I let my children decide where they wanted to go on the weekend. The children _____ all like to swim chose the beach.

7. Nations _____ are islands often have big fishing industries.

8. Japan _____ is an island-nation has a big fishing industry.

9. Bananas _____ are grown only in warm countries are quite nutritious.

10. My brother likes bananas _____ are grown in Taiwan the best.

11. On our hike, we took a bottle of water with us. The water _____ became warm as we were hiking didn't taste good.

12. International companies like to hire people _____ can speak at least two languages.

Exercise 4

Combine the sentences using **who**, **which**, or **that**.

1. The couple wanted to have children. They decided to adopt one.
   The couple <u>who</u> wanted to have children decided to adopt one.

2. We saw an accident. The accident was caused by a drunk driver.
   We saw an accident <u>which</u> was caused by a drunk driver.

3. The teenager felt bored. He painted graffiti on a train car.

   _____

4. There was some food in the garbage. The food was thrown away by a restaurant.

   _____

5. Our team is looking for a new coach. The new coach has professional experience.

   _____

Exercise 5

Write **OK** next to the sentences that are grammatically correct.

___ 1. My brother has an odd habit which is very annoying.

___ 2. My brother has an odd habit is very annoying.

___ 3. There are stereotypes can cause misunderstandings.

___ 4. There are stereotypes which can cause misunderstandings.

___ 5. The employee was very lazy often played video games during work.

___ 6. The employee who was very lazy often played video games during work.

___ 7. The most popular celebrities are the ones who give autographs to their fans.

___ 8. The most popular celebrities are the ones give autographs to their fans.

Exercise 6

   1) Write **S** above all the subjects and **V** above all the verbs.
   2) Add **who**, **which**, or **that** if necessary.

   S   **V**   *that* **V**
1. He often shops in a store Δ has cheap prices.

2. When I have a problem, I talk to my friend gives me advice.

3. There was a policeman came to our apartment.

4. The computers which have viruses need repairs.

5. There is a study shows that 70% of high school students have cheated at least once.

6. The second substance makes people feel shaky is caffeine.

7. There were a lot of people in my town have special artistic talents.

Exercise 7

   ❶ Write two sentences with restrictive clauses.
   ❷ Write two sentences with non-restrictive clauses.

_____

_____

_____

_____

Grammar Unit 11
Transitional Expressions and Conjunctions

• However,	• Moreover,	• so	• Therefore,
• and	• As a result,	• Nevertheless,	• In addition,
• but	• Furthermore,	• Consequently,	• Also,

Exercise 1

Fill in the blanks with the conjunctions and transitional expressions (conjunctive adverbs) in the box above.

Rule 1: These words can start sentences:

Transitional Expressions

- _____   - _____
- _____   - _____
- _____   - _____
- _____   - _____
- _____

Rule 2: These words <u>do not</u> usually start sentences. They combine sentences:

Conjunctions

- _____   - _____   - _____

Exercise 2

Write **OK** next to the sentences that follow the rules above.

___ 1. I like football. And, I like basketball.
___ 2. I like football. Also, I like basketball.

___ 3. He speaks Spanish, but I speak English.
___ 4. He speaks Spanish, however, I speak English.

___ 5. I'm not hungry, so I'll continue to study.
___ 6. I'm not hungry, therefore, I'll continue to study.

___ 7. Yesterday there was an accident near my house, and there was a fire.
___ 8. Yesterday there was an accident near my house, furthermore, there was a fire.

___ 9. My team lost the game. As a result, I was very upset.
___ 10. My team lost the game. And, I was very upset.

___ 11. There is a big test tomorrow. But, I am not ready for it.
___ 12. There is a big test tomorrow. However, I am not ready for it.

___ 13. The concert was canceled, consequently many people were disappointed.
___ 14. The concert was canceled. As a result, many people were disappointed.

Exercise 3: Look again at the list of expressions in the box on page 188.
Fill in the blanks in the box below with those expressions.

Conjunctions		Transitional Expressions
and	means the same as	*In addition* _____
		_____
		_____
		_____
but	means the same as	_____
		_____
so	means the same as	_____
		_____
		_____

Exercise 4

Choose the better expressions.

1. I like reading French books. [Furthermore / However], I enjoy listening to French music.

2. Because I live alone, I always cook my own meals. [Moreover / However], my mother does my laundry.

3. If it's cold tomorrow, I'll drive to work, [and / but] if it's warm, I'll ride my bike.

4. Marie hates flying in planes. [Also / Nevertheless], she must take one in order to get home.

5. I was feeling a lot of stress last week. [Nevertheless / As a result], I got the flu.

Exercise 5

Fill in the blanks with transitional expressions and conjunctions.

1. The boy studied all night for his test. _____, he didn't pass it.

2. The Japanese language uses a variety of complicated written characters. _____ _____, the Chinese language does too.

3. For a party, rock music is very nice, _____ for relaxing, people tend to prefer classical music.

4. I have to work today, _____ I must work tomorrow too.

Exercise 6

Complete the sentences.

1. Yesterday was a terrible day. In the morning, I was late and missed the bus. *Furthermore,* _____

   _____

2. School life has some good and bad points. It is fine because students learn new things every day.

   Nevertheless, _____

   _____

3. This school is a very interesting place. The students are all very charming. *In addition,* _____

   _____

   _____

4. This school is a very interesting place. The students are all very charming. *However,* _____

   _____

   _____

5. Gina would like to take a trip to Asia next year. *Consequently,* _____

   _____

   _____

Exercise 7

Complete these sentences with the correct punctuation and a conjunction or transitional expression.

1. I would like to travel around the world. *Therefore, I am saving money and studying a foreign language.*

2. My sister doesn't eat meat*, but she loves vegetables.* _____

3. Children nowadays watch too much television _____

4. They say that Canada is a good place to spend a vacation _____

5. American movies show a lot of action _____

6. My brother has to get up at 5:30 a.m. for work on weekdays _____

7. Scientists today say that smoking hurts our health _____

Grammar Unit 12
Review I

(Transitional expressions and conjunctions / clauses / reduced clauses)

Directions

Read these directions and questions about the worksheet below to your partners.

1. Look at Sentence A. Is there a problem with the word "also" in this sentence? Why? If you need help, look at Unit 11.
4. Look at Sentence B. If we want to use a conjunction, what needs to be changed?
7. Look at Sentence D. Reduce the dependent clause to a phrase if it is possible. If you need help, look at Unit 9.
10. Look at Sentence F. Underline the dependent clause.
13. Look at H. Underline the dependent clauses.
16. Look at Sentence I. How can we improve this sentence?
19. Look at Sentence J. If we need commas, put them in. If you need help, look at Unit 10.
22. Look at Sentence K. If we need commas, put them in.
25. Look at Sentence L. Did you put in three commas?
28. Look at Sentence N. If we need commas, put them in.

Worksheet

A. During our trip, we visited a castle, also, we went to a museum.

B. Tom was in a great hurry to get to work this morning. _____, he forgot to lock the door to his apartment.

C. Her dinner was very salty. _____, she drank a lot of water afterwards.

D. Before he started to climb the mountain, he checked the weather report.

E. Some people talk on a cell-phone while they are driving.

F. My uncle was very proud after his daughter won the beauty contest.

G. When Ken arrived at the beach he put on suntan lotion because he didn't want to get a sunburn.

H. Although she is allergic to cheese which is made from goat's milk.

I. My brother doubts her to go to the party with him.

J. The policeman who caught the thief received a reward.

K. The American flag which is red, white, and blue looks like the Liberian flag.

L. Before she began her tennis match my oldest sister who is a great player felt nervous because she broke a string on her favorite racket.

M. I hope that my newspaper will tell the story about the restaurant, which served the stale fish.

N. If Tom wins the lottery he plans to travel to Ireland which has some famous castles.

B

Review I • Directions
(Transitional expressions and conjunctions / clauses / reduced clauses)

Read these directions and questions about the worksheet below to your partners.

2. Look at Sentence A. If I want to use a comma after the word "castle," what word should I write after it?

5. Look at Sentence C. Should we write "Furthermore" or "Consequently" in the blank?

8. Look at Sentence E. Underline the dependent clause.

11. Look at Sentence F. If possible, reduce the dependent clause to a phrase.

14. In H, is there a problem? Explain. Also, how can we correct it?

17. Look at Sentence J. Underline the dependent clause.

20. Look at Sentence K. Underline the dependent clause.

23. Look at Sentence L. Underline the three dependent clauses.

26. Look at Sentence M. Are the commas used correctly in this sentence?

29. Look at Sentence N. Did you put in two commas?

Worksheet

A. During our trip, we visited a castle, also, we went to a museum.

B. Tom was in a great hurry to get to work this morning. _____, he forgot to lock the door to his apartment.

C. Her dinner was very salty. _____, she drank a lot of water afterwards.

D. Before he started to climb the mountain, he checked the weather report.

E. Some people talk on a cell-phone while they are driving.

F. My uncle was very proud after his daughter won the beauty contest.

G. When Ken arrived at the beach he put on suntan lotion because he didn't want to get a sunburn.

H. Although she is allergic to cheese which is made from goat's milk.

I. My brother doubts her to go to the party with him.

J. The policeman who caught the thief received a reward.

K. The American flag which is red, white, and blue looks like the Liberian flag.

L. Before she began her tennis match my oldest sister who is a great player felt nervous because she broke a string on her favorite racket.

M. I hope that my newspaper will tell the story about the restaurant, which served the stale fish.

N. If Tom wins the lottery he plans to travel to Ireland which has some famous castles.

Review I • Directions
(Transitional expressions and conjunctions / clauses / reduced clauses)

Read these directions and questions about the worksheet below to your partners.

3. Look at Sentence B. What transitional expressions could we write in the blank?
6. Look at Sentence D. Underline the dependent clause.
9. Look at Sentence E. Is it possible to reduce the dependent clause to a phrase even though it comes at the end of the sentence?
12. Look at Sentence G. Underline the two dependent clauses. Also, put in a comma.
15. Look at Sentence I. Are we supposed to use a dependent clause after the verb "doubt"? If you need help, look at Unit 8.
18. Look at Sentence J. Is the dependent clause necessary or extra information?
21. Look at Sentence K. Is the dependent clause necessary or extra information?
24. Look at Sentence L. Put in any commas if they are needed.
27. Look at Sentence N. Underline the two dependent clauses.

Worksheet

A. During our trip, we visited a castle, also, we went to a museum.
B. Tom was in a great hurry to get to work this morning. _____, he forgot to lock the door to his apartment.
C. Her dinner was very salty. _____, she drank a lot of water afterwards.
D. Before he started to climb the mountain, he checked the weather report.
E. Some people talk on a cell-phone while they are driving.
F. My uncle was very proud after his daughter won the beauty contest.
G. When Ken arrived at the beach he put on suntan lotion because he didn't want to get a sunburn.
H. Although she is allergic to cheese which is made from goat's milk.
I. My brother doubts her to go to the party with him.
J. The policeman who caught the thief received a reward.
K. The American flag which is red, white, and blue looks like the Liberian flag.
L. Before she began her tennis match my oldest sister who is a great player felt nervous because she broke a string on her favorite racket.
M. I hope that my newspaper will tell the story about the restaurant, which served the stale fish.
N. If Tom wins the lottery he plans to travel to Ireland which has some famous castles.

Grammar Unit 13
Commas (,) and Semicolons (;)

Exercise 1

❶ Look at the sample sentences below.
❷ For the rules about commas, fill in the blanks with words in the box.

> • introductory phrase*___ • conjunction ___ • transitional expression _X_
>
> • dependent ___ • independent ___
>
> * Very short phrases of three words or less may not need a comma.

General rules for commas

1. Sample sentence: *Therefore, she canceled her appointment.*
   Rule 1: Put a comma after a _transitional expression_

2. Sample sentence: *It began to snow, so we decided to stay home.*
   Rule 2: Put a comma before a _____ that joins
   two _____ clauses.

3. Sample sentence: *After Tom found a seat on the subway, he started to read.*
   Rule 3: Put a comma after a _____ clause that starts a sentence.

4. Sample sentence: *Next to the phone in the kitchen, you will find some paper to write on.*
   Rule 4: Put a comma after an _____.

Exercise 2

❶ Look at the sample mistakes below.
❷ For the rules about common mistakes, fill in the blanks with words in the box.

> • an independent clause ___ • a subordinator ___ • subject and verb ___ • verbs ___

Common mistakes with commas

1. Sample mistake: *She went to the theater, and bought a ticket.*
   Correct: *She went to the theater and bought a ticket.*
   Rule 5: Don't put a comma when you have two _____ but only one subject.

2. Sample mistake: *My dog started to bark, when the door bell rang.*
   Correct: *My dog started to bark when the door bell rang.*
   Rule 6: Don't put a comma after _____ which starts your sentence.

3. Sample mistake: *Although, the shoes were cheap, he didn't buy any.*
   Correct: *Although the shoes were cheap, he didn't buy any.*
   Rule 7: Don't put a comma after _____.

4. Sample mistake: *The man in the front row, is my boss.*
   Correct: *The man in the front row is my boss.*
   Rule 8: Don't put a comma between the _____.

Exercise 3

❶ Look at the sample sentences below.
❷ For the rules about semicolons, fill in the blanks with words in the box.

• dependent ___ • independent ___ • independent ___

General rules for semicolons

1. Correct sample sentence: *The team played well. However, they lost.*
   Correct sample sentence: *The team played well; however, they lost.*
   Rule 9: You can put a semicolon between two _____ clauses.

2. Sample mistake: *Because there was a problem; we had to work late.*
   Correct sample sentence: *Because there was a problem, we had to work late.*
   Rule 10: Don't put a semicolon between a _____ and
   _____ clause.

Exercise 4

Put in <u>eight commas and two semicolons</u> in the sentences below.

1. We were hungry but didn't have time to eat.
2. Although the doctor was on vacation she said that I could call her.
3. Bill's suitcase was small. Therefore he wasn't able to pack all of his sweaters.
4. Inside the envelope which is over there you will find some money.
5. After I heard the answer I felt more confident.
6. The runners forgot to stretch before the race so their muscles soon began to hurt.
7. The team did a lot better during the second half of the game.
8. We parked at the airport and took a plane to Seattle.
9. My older brother likes rock music my younger brother prefers classical.
10. When the letter arrived she quickly tore it open.
11. The computer with the extra-large screen is the best one for this project.
12. Tom had to sell his dog because his children were afraid of it.
13. Because of the heavy traffic we stayed home.
14. He played in a band however it never became famous.

Grammar Unit 14
Gerunds and Participles

Gerund = <u>Verb</u> + *ing* used as a noun

I enjoy **reading.**

Reading is easier than **writing.**

Exercise 1

Gerunds used as subjects:

❶ Underline the gerunds.
❷ Write **S** above the subjects.
❸ Write **V** above the verbs and **AV** above the auxiliary verbs.

          ^S   ^{AV} ^V

Example: <u>Driving</u> during a storm can be a challenge.

1. Writing a good introduction will get the reader's attention.

2. Signing autographs is a common activity for celebrities. (**Note**: *Gerunds take singular verbs.*)

3. Eating in restaurants has some advantages over eating at home.

4. Drinking bottled water is usually safe.

Exercise 2

Gerunds that come after prepositions are objects of prepositions

❶ (Circle) the prepositions.
❷ Underline the gerunds.

Example: My brother is good (at) <u>fixing</u> computers.

1. We complained to our neighbor because we were tired of listening to all the noise.

2. His boss talked to him about finishing the project.

Exercise 3

Note: Sometimes a <u>verb</u>-*ing* is not a gerund (noun). It can be a present participle that is an adjective. (An adjective describes a noun.)

• Write *gerund* or *participle* for each underlined word.

_____ 1. <u>Traveling</u> all over Europe helped Tom understand some new cultures.

_____ 2. The <u>crying</u> baby alerted us to the problem.

_____ 3. We got little sleep last night because of the <u>barking</u> dog.

_____/_____ 4. They insisted on <u>singing</u> even though I said that <u>dancing</u> is more fun.

_____ 5. I celebrated last night when I learned that I had the <u>winning</u> ticket.

Exercise 4

Write three sentences with a gerund as the subject.

_____

_____

_____

Exercise 5

❶ Write three sentences with a preposition and gerund in a prepositional phrase.

❷ (Circle) the prepositions

❸ <u>Underline</u> the gerunds.

_____

_____

_____

Exercise 6

Write sentences using the cues.

Example: (cue: working + noun) <u>Working mothers</u> sometimes need help with child care.
                            (participle) (noun)

Example: (cue: frightening + noun) I seldom watch <u>frightening movies</u> at night.
                                           (participle) (noun)

1. cue: falling   leaves:
   (participle) (noun)

2. cue: burning _____:
   (participle) (noun)

3. cue: smoking _____:
   (participle) (noun)

4. cue: crying _____:
   (participle) (noun)

Grammar Unit 15
Infinitives

Infinitive = to + verb

Exercise 1

<u>Underline</u> the infinitives.

Example: <u>To get</u> her attention is sometimes difficult.

1. After dinner, I want you to repair the TV.
2. Jill decided to buy some new furniture.
3. The poet began to read a poem to the audience.

Exercise 2

"To" can be a part of the *infinitive* or a *preposition*.

❶ Write **I** above the "to" if it is part of an infinitive.
❷ Write **P** above the "to" if it is a preposition.

Example: The first baby <u>to</u> arrive in the New Year is always given special attention.

1. After Bill's school term ended, his parents took him <u>to</u> an amusement park.
2. We are planning <u>to</u> send the information <u>to</u> our parents via e-mail.
3. When the crowd started <u>to</u> become restless, the police were sent <u>to</u> the area <u>to</u> try <u>to</u> control them.

Exercise 3

Sometimes the infinitive can be the subject of the sentence.

❶ Underline the subjects of the sentences.
❷ Circle the verbs of the sentences and write **AV** above the auxiliary verbs.

Example 1: <u>To impress</u> our parents (is) sometimes difficult. (**Note**: *Infinitives take a **singular verb**.)*

Example 2: To get strong muscles, <u>Tom</u> (lifts) weights three times a week.

1. To learn how to drive well requires a lot of practice.
2. To learn how to drive well, Tom enrolled in a driving school.
3. To find a roommate, we can put an ad in the newspaper.
4. To use infinitives correctly is not always easy.
5. To find a cure for the disease, doctors are experimenting with rats.
6. To find a cure for the disease is the doctor's top priority.
7. To be a successful writer became his biggest goal.
8. To leave immediately seemed the best thing to do.

After some verbs, we use <u>gerunds</u> and after other verbs, we use <u>infinitives</u>. Some verbs can take either a gerund or an infinitive.

V + gerund	V + infinitive	V + gerund or infinitive
admit	appear	attempt
consider	ask	begin
dislike	claim	hate
enjoy	decide	like
finish	hope	love
miss	promise	prefer
practice	refuse	start
recommend	want	stop

Exercise 4

Write the correct forms of the verbs in the blanks.

Example: My roommate admitted ___*taking*___ (take) the last piece of pizza.

1. If you know anyone who wants _____ (perform) at the festival, tell them that they should consider _____ (practice) with us.
2. Because of our muddy shoes, we were asked _____ (take) them off before entering the room.
3. My friend hopes _____ (get) medical treatment for his leg.
4. The travel agent recommends _____ (apply) for a visa two months in advance.

Exercise 5

❶ Write two sentences with an infinitive. Use verbs from the box above. Put the infinitives after the verbs.
❷ <u>Underline</u> the infinitives.

Exercise 6

❶ Write two sentences with the preposition "to."
❷ <u>Underline</u> the prepositions.

Exercise 7

❶ Write one sentence with an infinitive as the subject of the sentence.
❷ <u>Underline</u> the infinitive.

Grammar Unit 16
Gerunds and Infinitives

Directions

Read these directions and questions about the worksheet below to your partners.

1. In Sentence A, underline the gerund.
4. In Sentence C, what is the subject?
7. In Sentence D, underline the gerund.
10. In Sentence E, what is the subject of the sentence?
13. In Sentence G, is "in marathons" the subject of the sentence?
16. In Sentence H, is the word "to" a preposition or part of an infinitive?

Worksheet

A. Starting a car in winter can be difficult.

B. Translating is a way for bilingual students to earn extra money.

C. Having exams before the holidays are difficult.

D. The tourists asked some questions about renting a car.

E. To become a doctor requires five years of medical school.

F. He decided to get a haircut.

G. To run in marathons successfully takes a lot of training.

H. After she went to the concert, she took a taxi home.

I. They enjoyed to watch the videos.

J. She is upset at me because I refused helping her.

Gerunds and Infinitives: Directions

Read these directions and questions about the worksheet below to your partners.

2. In Sentence B, underline the subject. Is it a gerund?
5. In Sentence C, what is the verb?
8. In Sentence D, is the gerund the subject of the sentence?
11. In Sentence F, is "to get" an infinitive or a prepositional phrase?
14. In Sentence G, what is the verb?
17. In Sentence I, is there a problem? Explain.

Worksheet

A. Starting a car in winter can be difficult.

B. Translating is a way for bilingual students to earn extra money.

C. Having exams before the holidays are difficult.

D. The tourists asked some questions about renting a car.

E. To become a doctor requires five years of medical school.

F. He decided to get a haircut.

G. To run in marathons successfully takes a lot of training.

H. After she went to the concert, she took a taxi home.

I. They enjoyed to watch the videos.

J. She is upset at me because I refused helping her.

Gerunds and Infinitives: Directions

Read these directions and questions about the worksheet below to your partners.

3. In Sentence B, is there an infinitive somewhere in this sentence?

6. In Sentence C, should the verb be "is"? Why or why not?

9. In Sentence D, why do we have a gerund after "about"?

12. In Sentence G, is "in marathons" a prepositional phrase?

15. In Sentence G, should the word "takes" be changed to "take"?

18. In Sentence J, is the word "helping" used correctly here? Explain.

Worksheet

A. Starting a car in winter can be difficult.

B. Translating is a way for bilingual students to earn extra money.

C. Having exams before the holidays are difficult.

D. The tourists asked some questions about renting a car.

E. To become a doctor requires five years of medical school.

F. He decided to get a haircut.

G. To run in marathons successfully takes a lot of training.

H. After she went to the concert, she took a taxi home.

I. They enjoyed to watch the videos.

J. She is upset at me because I refused helping her.

Grammar Unit 17
Conditional Sentences

Type I. Real: The situation *very possibly* **will happen.**

• get	• will take	• is	• will eat
• conditional	• future	• past	• present

Exercise 1:

Fill in the blanks in the Examples 1 and 2 below and Rule One with words from the box above. (You will not use all the words in the box.)

Example 1. If the moon _____ full tonight, everyone _____ a walk in the moonlight.

Example 2. Today, I _____ a snack, if I _____ hungry.

Rule One: If the dependent clause is _____ tense, then the independent clause is _____ tense.

Type II. Unreal: It *probably* or *certainly* **will not happen.**

• would pay	• attended	• would live	• won
• conditional	• future	• past	• present

Exercise 2

Fill in the blanks in the Examples 3 and 4 below and Rule Two with words from the box above. (You will not use all the words in the box.)

Example 3: If he _____ the lottery tomorrow, he _____ all his bills.

Example 4. Most community college students live either at home or in an apartment. If these students _____ a university instead of a community college, many of them _____ in a dormitory.

Rule Two: If the dependent clause is _____ tense, then the independent clause is _____ tense.

Exercise 3: Circle the sentence in each pair that is grammatically correct.

1. (a) If Sara gets a low grade on her exam, she will ask her instructor for extra help.
   (b) If Sara will get a low grade on her exam, she will ask her instructor for extra help.

2. (a) If cigarettes are banned, people would have fewer health problems.
   (b) If cigarettes were banned, people would have fewer health problems.

3. (a) If scientists used animals for research, the animals will suffer.
   (b) If scientists use animals for research, the animals will suffer.

4. (a) If a huge asteroid crashed into the world, it would destroy life here.
   (b) If a huge asteroid would crash into the world, it would destroy life here.

Type III. Unreal: **It** is *too late*, so it **cannot happen.**

> • had studied   • hadn't hurt   • would have become
> • would have received   • injured
> • past conditional   • past   • past perfect   • present perfect

Exercise 4: Fill in the blanks in the Examples 5 and 6 below and Rule Three with words from the box above. (You will not use all the words in the box.)

Example 5: If I _____ harder in elementary school, I _____ better grades.

Example 6: Ken _____ his leg playing tennis, so he stopped playing. He _____ _____ a professional player if he _____ his leg.

Rule Three: If the dependent clause is _____ tense, then the independent clause is _____ tense.

Exercise 5: Circle the sentence in each pair that is grammatically correct.

1. (a) If I remembered her name, I would have asked her for a date.
   (b) If I had remembered her name, I would have asked her for a date.

2. (a) Tim would have taken a vacation if his boss had given him a pay raise.
   (b) Tim would take a vacation if his boss had given him a pay raise.

3. (a) If she had asked a question, she would avoid that foolish mistake.
   (b) If she had asked a question, she would have avoided that foolish mistake.

Exercise 6 Complete the sentences.

1. If my cellphone rings during my class right now, _____
   _____

2. He is in the hospital now. He wouldn't have become sick if _____
   _____

3. We would spend more time with our neighbors if _____
   _____

4. If I married someone from a foreign country, my parents _____
   _____

5. If I had been more confident in the past, _____
   _____

6. She will be happy to help you if _____
   _____

A

Unit 18 Group Work • Student

Section 3: Grammar

Grammar Unit 18
Reduced Adjective Clauses

Directions

Read these directions and questions about the worksheet below to your partners.

1. Look at Sentence A. Underline the dependent clause "who is talking to my brother."
4. Look at Sentence D. Underline the dependent clause "that was taken from me on the subway."
7. In Sentence G, underline the dependent clause. Then on Line H, complete the sentence by changing the clause to a phrase.
10. In Sentence K, change the clause to a phrase. To do this, you need to change the form of the word "want." Re-write the sentence on Line L.
13. In Sentence M, change the clause to a phrase by taking out the words "who does." To do so, you must also change the form of the word "want." Re-write the sentence on Line N.
16. In Sentence Q, is there a problem?
19. In Sentence V, complete the sentence and include a phrase.

Worksheet

A. I know the man who is talking to my brother.
B. Reduce clause to a phrase: _____
C. _____
D. They found the watch that was taken from me on the subway. (Notice passive form.)
E. _____
F. _____
G. The plane that is going to Chicago is delayed.
H. The plane _____ is delayed.
I. My employer bought a house which was built in 1820. (Notice passive form.)
J. _____
K. Any student who wants to pass this course must write a research paper.
L. _____
M. Any student who does not want to fail must attend class regularly.
N. _____
O. The actor who was given the award lives near my house.
P. _____
Q. The student wait for the Internet needs help.
R. Customers who are not wearing shoes will not be allowed to enter the cafe.
S. _____
T. We shouldn't eat the fish which were caught in that river because of the pollution.
U. _____
V. I'd like to talk to that girl _____
W. He showed everyone a tree planted by his great-grandfather.
X. _____
Y. The children playing in her garden make her angry.
Z. _____

206 • **Grammar Unit 18:** *Reduced Adjective Clauses*

Reduced Adjective Clauses: Directions

Read these directions and questions about the worksheet below to your partners.

2. On Line B, reduce the clause to a phrase. Write the words "talking to my brother" on this line.
5. On Line E, change the clause to a phrase. Write the words "taken from me on the subway."
8. In Sentence I, underline the dependent clause. Then re-write the sentence on Line J by changing the clause to a phrase.
11. In Sentence L, did you change the word "wants" to "wanting"?
14. In Sentence N, did you change the words "who does not want" to the words "not wanting"?
17. In Sentence R, how can we change the clause to a phrase? Write on Line S.
20. In Sentence W, this time, change the phrase to a clause. Re-write the sentence on Line X.

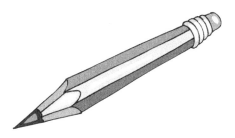

Worksheet

A. I know the man who is talking to my brother.
B. Reduce clause to a phrase: _____
C. _____
D. They found the watch that was taken from me on the subway. (Notice passive form.)
E. _____
F. _____
G. The plane that is going to Chicago is delayed.
H. The plane _____ is delayed.
I. My employer bought a house which was built in 1820. (Notice passive form.)
J. _____
K. Any student who wants to pass this course must write a research paper.
L. _____
M. Any student who does not want to fail must attend class regularly.
N. _____
O. The actor who was given the award lives near my house.
P. _____
Q. The student wait for the Internet needs help.
R. Customers who are not wearing shoes will not be allowed to enter the cafe.
S. _____
T. We shouldn't eat the fish which were caught in that river because of the pollution.
U. _____
V. I'd like to talk to that girl _____
W. He showed everyone a tree planted by his great-grandfather.
X. _____
Y. The children playing in her garden make her angry.
Z. _____

B

C

Reduced Adjective Clauses: Directions

Read these directions and questions about the worksheet below to your partners.

3. On Line C, write the complete sentence with the clause reduced to a phrase: "I know the man talking to my brother."
6. On Line F, write the complete sentence with the clause reduced to a phrase: "They found the watch taken from me on the subway." Notice the correct word is "taken," not "taking."
9. In Sentence K, underline the dependent clause.
12. In Sentence M, underline the dependent clause.
15. In Sentence O, change the clause to a phrase. Re-write the sentence on Line P.
18. In Sentence T, change the clause to a phrase and re-write the sentence on Line U.
21. In Sentence Y, change the phrase to a clause. Re-write the sentence on Line Z.

Worksheet

A. I know the man who is talking to my brother.
B. Reduce clause to a phrase: _____
C. _____
D. They found the watch that was taken from me on the subway. (Notice passive form.)
E. _____
F. _____
G. The plane that is going to Chicago is delayed.
H. The plane _____ is delayed.
I. My employer bought a house which was built in 1820. (Notice passive form.)
J. _____
K. Any student who wants to pass this course must write a research paper.
L. _____
M. Any student who does not want to fail must attend class regularly.
N. _____
O. The actor who was given the award lives near my house.
P. _____
Q. The student wait for the Internet needs help.
R. Customers who are not wearing shoes will not be allowed to enter the cafe.
S. _____
T. We shouldn't eat the fish which were caught in that river because of the pollution.
U. _____
V. I'd like to talk to that girl _____
W. He showed everyone a tree planted by his great-grandfather.
X. _____
Y. The children playing in her garden make her angry.
Z. _____

Grammar Unit 19
Reduced Adjective Clauses

Exercise 1

❶ Underline the dependent clauses.
❷ On the line below each sentence, change the dependent clause to a phrase.

1. A policeman who was driving an unmarked car gave me a speeding ticket.

   _____

2. Only the workers who were given a raise were celebrating.

   _____

3. The tour that is taking us to Greece is full.

   _____

4. The voters who want a new president decided to form a committee.

   _____

5. Any letter that does not have a stamp on it will be returned to the sender.

   _____

Exercise 2

❶ Use the cues and write sentences with a clause with **who**, **which**, or **that**.
❷ Write the same sentences but, in each, change the clause to a phrase.

Example:

cue: *small child—cry*

• *(Sentence with a clause):* The police found a small child who was crying for his mother.

• *(Sentence with a phrase):* The police found a small child crying for his mother.

1. **cue**: *cowboy — sit*
   • *(Sentence with a clause):* _____
   • *(Sentence with a phrase):* _____

2. **cue**: *students — use*
   • *(Sentence with a clause):* _____
   • *(Sentence with a phrase):* _____

3. **cue**: *woman — talk*
   • *(Sentence with a clause):* _____
   • *(Sentence with a phrase):* _____

Exercise 3

❶ Write two sentences including a clause with **who**, **which**, or **that**.
❷ Write the same sentences again but, in each, change the clause to a phrase.

Grammar Unit 20
Adjective Clauses Reduced to Prepositional Phrases

Examples:

  a. Underline the dependent clause.
  • *The house that is **on the corner** was hit by lightning.*

  b. Change the clause to a prepositional phrase, and write the whole sentence again.
  • *The house **on the corner** was hit by lightening.*

Exercise 1

1. a. Underline the dependent clause.
   • *The passenger who is sitting in the front seat should study the map.*
   b. Change the clause to a prepositional phrase and write the whole sentence again.
   The girl with _____

2. a. Underline the dependent clause.
   • *The girl who is wearing the headband is a great athlete.*
   b. Change the clause to a prepositional phrase using the preposition **"with"** and write the whole sentence again.
   _____

3. a. Underline the dependent clause.
   • *We always buy our fruit from the store which is near our house.*
   b. Change the clause to a prepositional phrase and write the whole sentence again.
   _____

4. a. Underline the dependent clause.
   • *If you meet the man who is wearing the red sweater, ask him for his autograph.*
   b. Change the clause to a prepositional phrase using the preposition **"in"** and write the whole sentence again.
   _____

5. a. Underline the dependent clause.
   • *My aunt likes to talk to people who come from foreign countries.*
   b. Change the clause to a prepositional phrase and write the whole sentence again.
   _____

6. a. Underline the dependent clause.
   - *There was a large fire in the city that is next to mine.*
   b. Change the clause to a prepositional phrase and write the whole sentence again.

   _____

Exercise 2

Complete the sentences and include a prepositional phrase.

1. I really don't want to sit near the man with _____

   _____

2. The box in _____

   _____

3. After he did his shopping at the store next to _____

   _____

Exercise 3: Write three sentences. For each:

❶ Write a sentence with an adjective clause that includes a prepositional phrase.
❷ Underline the adjective clause.
❸ Re-write the sentence with the clause reduced to a prepositional phrase.
❹ Circle the prepositions. *(See the list of prepositions on page 173.)*

Example:

I bought a picture that was (by) my favorite artist.

I bought a picture by my favorite artist.

_____

_____

_____

_____

_____

_____

Grammar Unit 21

Sentences with Initial Modifying Phrases

[adjective (adj) + preposition (p)]

Example 1:

                        adj p

                We were **tired of waiting**, <u>so</u> we decided to leave.

(modifying phrase) ~~We were~~ <u>tired of waiting</u>, ~~so~~ …

       Sentence: ***Tired of waiting***, *we decided to leave.*

Example 2:

                        adj   p

            The team was **happy about the score**, <u>so</u> they celebrated.

(modifying phrase) ~~The team was~~ <u>happy about the score</u>, ~~so~~ …

       Sentence: ***Happy about the score***, *the team celebrated.*

Exercise 1

❶ Write **adj** above the adjectives.

❷ Write **p** above the prepositions that come after the adjectives.

❸ Reduce the first subject and verb in each sentence to a modifying phrase.

1. My father was sick with the flu, so he stayed home from work.

    _____

2. We were excited about our plans, so we drove all night.

    _____

3. The hiker was exhausted by the climb, so he lay down and fell asleep.

    _____

4. Some students were bored by the lecture, so they left early.

    _____

5. I was disappointed with my test scores, so I decided to study harder.

    _____

Example 3:

adj   p

He refused to own a car <u>because</u> he was **afraid of driving**.

(modifying phrase) ~~He was~~ <u>afraid of driving</u>, ~~because~~ …

Sentence: **Afraid of driving**, he refused to own a car.

Example 4:

adj   p

<u>Because</u> she was **pleased with the results**, she laughed hard.

(modifying phrase) ~~Because she was~~ <u>pleased with the results</u>.

Sentence: **Pleased with the results**, she laughed hard.

Exercise 2

❶ Write **adj** above the adjectives.
❷ Write **p** above the prepositions.
❸ Reduce the "because" clauses in each sentence to include an initial modifying phrase.

1. <u>Because</u> he was shocked by his son's grades, the father wouldn't let his son watch TV.

_____

2. My brother decided not to accept the job offer <u>because</u> he was worried about the low salary.

_____

Exercise 3

❶ Choose <u>four of the phrases</u> in the box below.
❷ Write sentences with the adjective followed by a prepositional phrase and "so" or "because," like those in Exercise 1 and Exercise 2 above.
❸ Write **adj** above the adjectives.
❹ Write **p** above the prepositions that come after the adjectives.
❺ <u>Underline</u> "so" or "because."
❻ Reduce the necessary parts to modifying phrases, as you did in Exercise 1 and Exercise 2.

• surprised by	• upset at	• proud of	• pleased with
• sad about	• satisfied with	• amused by	• embarrassed by
• confused by (about)	• frightened by	• curious about	• thrilled with

A

Unit 22 Group Work • Student

Section 3: Grammar

Grammar Unit 22
Commas and Semicolons

Directions

Read these directions and questions about the worksheet below to your partners.

1. Look at Sentence A. Should we put a comma in this sentence? Why or why not?
4. In Sentence D, is there a problem with the comma? Explain.
7. In Sentence G, could we put a period here instead of a semicolon? Why or why not?
10. In Sentence J, do you see anything wrong with the comma? Explain.
13. Look at Sentence M. Should we put a comma in this sentence? Why or why not?

Worksheet

A. Therefore the car got a flat tire.

B. While we were on the ship we saw some whales.

C. Her horse won the prize so, they decided to celebrate.

D. As the years passed, the couple began to find new friends.

E. The stewardess let the passengers board the plane, when the snow stopped falling outside.

F. Although, our 2-week vacation is coming soon, I have no plans yet.

G. Someone stole Ken's passport; in addition, he lost his credit cards.

H. They found a beautiful area, and built their house there.

I. The man talking on the cell phone, told me about a good restaurant.

J. After seeing a movie about Africa, Sue decided to take a trip there.

K. Tom usually studies in his apartment his roommate does his homework in the library.

L. We need to fill the gas tank and we should also check the tires.

M. Because I have an unusual name nobody knows how to pronounce it correctly.

N. His mother hid the presents inside the closet; because she didn't want the children to find them.

O. In 15 minutes, the bus should arrive.

Commas and Semicolons: Directions

Read these directions and questions about the worksheet below to your partners.

2. Look at Sentence B. Should we put a comma in this sentence? Why or why not?
5. In Sentence E, do you see anything wrong with the comma? Explain.
8. In Sentence H, do we need a comma here? Explain.
11. In Sentence K, should we put a comma or a semicolon in this? Explain.
14. In Sentence N, is the semicolon used correctly here? Explain.

Worksheet

A. Therefore the car got a flat tire.

B. While we were on the ship we saw some whales.

C. Her horse won the prize so, they decided to celebrate.

D. As the years passed, the couple began to find new friends.

E. The stewardess let the passengers board the plane, when the snow stopped falling outside.

F. Although, our 2-week vacation is coming soon, I have no plans yet.

G. Someone stole Ken's passport; in addition, he lost his credit cards.

H. They found a beautiful area, and built their house there.

I. The man talking on the cell phone, told me about a good restaurant.

J. After seeing a movie about Africa, Sue decided to take a trip there.

K. Tom usually studies in his apartment his roommate does his homework in the library.

L. We need to fill the gas tank and we should also check the tires.

M. Because I have an unusual name nobody knows how to pronounce it correctly.

N. His mother hid the presents inside the closet; because she didn't want the children to find them.

O. In 15 minutes, the bus should arrive.

Commas and Semicolons: Directions

Read these directions and questions about the worksheet below to your partners.

3. Look at Sentence C. Do you see anything wrong with the comma? Explain.
6. In Sentence F, is there something wrong with one of the comma? Explain.
9. In Sentence I, is there a problem with the comma? Explain.
12. In Sentence L, should we put in a comma? Why or why not?
15. In Sentence O, do you see anything wrong with the comma? Explain.

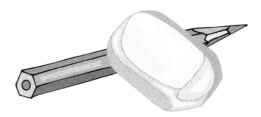

Worksheet

A. Therefore the car got a flat tire.

B. While we were on the ship we saw some whales.

C. Her horse won the prize so, they decided to celebrate.

D. As the years passed, the couple began to find new friends.

E. The stewardess let the passengers board the plane, when the snow stopped falling outside.

F. Although, our 2-week vacation is coming soon, I have no plans yet.

G. Someone stole Ken's passport; in addition, he lost his credit cards.

H. They found a beautiful area, and built their house there.

I. The man talking on the cell phone, told me about a good restaurant.

J. After seeing a movie about Africa, Sue decided to take a trip there.

K. Tom usually studies in his apartment his roommate does his homework in the library.

L. We need to fill the gas tank and we should also check the tires.

M. Because I have an unusual name nobody knows how to pronounce it correctly.

N. His mother hid the presents inside the closet; because she didn't want the children to find them.

O. In 15 minutes, the bus should arrive.

Grammar Unit 23
Practice with Adjectives

Exercise 1: Correct the adjectives that are mistakenly used as verbs.

❶ Write **V** above the verbs and **adj** above the adjectives in the underlined sections.
❷ Write **Right** if the verbs and adjectives are used correctly (There is a total of four.)
❸ Write **Wrong** if the verbs and adjectives are used incorrectly. (There is a total of six.)
❹ If there is a mistake, write the sentence correctly.

Right 1. She comes from a beautiful country.
                V   adj
       Correction: *none*

Right 2. The patient was frightened by the doctor's report.
                  V   adj
       Correction: *none*

Wrong 3. Ken exercised for two hours, so now he tired.
                                 adj
       Correction: *Ken exercised for two hours, so now he is tired.*

_____ 4. Our vacation was ruined because the weather was terrible.
       Correction: _____

_____ 5. They confused by the menu, which was in a foreign language.
       Correction: _____

_____ 6. When Ann heard the news, she shocked.
       Correction: _____

_____ 7. Tom needed some help, but he was afraid to tell anyone.
       Correction: _____

_____ 8. At the zoo, the children disappointed because the lions were all sleeping.
       Correction: _____

_____ 9. I surprised at how long his hair was.
       Correction: _____

_____ 10. Ann won the music award, so her parents proud of her.
       Correction: _____

Exercise 2: Adjective-*ing* and Adjective-*ed*

> *Usually*:
>
> • <u>people</u> are adjective-<u>*ed*</u>. (*Tom was confused.*)
>
> • <u>things</u> are adjective-<u>*ing*</u>. (*This <u>book</u> is confus<u>ing</u>.*)

❶ (Circle) the word that is described.
❷ Write **Right** if adjectives are used correctly (There are two.)
❸ Write **Wrong** if the adjectives are used incorrectly.
❹ If there is a mistake, change it.

Wrong 1. After he tore his pants, (Tom) felt embarrassing. *embarrassed*

_____ 2. My father thinks that shopping is <u>boring</u>.

_____ 3. I was <u>exciting</u> when I heard that it would snow the next day.

_____ 4. We couldn't sleep in that hotel because the noise was <u>frightened</u>.

_____ 5. Dan decided not to go there because, the last time, he felt <u>disappointed</u>.

_____ 6. Most of the students are <u>interesting</u> in their scores.

Grammar Unit 24

Review II

**(Restrictive/Non-restrictive clauses / noun clauses /
reduced adjective clauses / modifying phrases)**

Directions

Read these directions and questions about the worksheet below to your partners.

1. Look at Sentence A. Put in commas if we need them. If you need help, see Unit 10.
4. Look at Sentence C. Put in commas if we need them.
7. Look at Sentence E. Underline the dependent clause.
10. Look at Sentence F. Reduce the dependent clause to a prepositional phrase.
13. Look at Sentence G. Reduce the dependent clause to a prepositional phrase.
16. In J, write a sentence that starts with the modifying phrase, "Satisfied with."

Worksheet

A. The woman who won the award for "Best Actress" had graduated from my college.

B. Every Sunday, Bill buys a New York Times which is one of the most popular newspapers in the country.

C. My brother is looking for a job which will earn him a lot of money, but he doesn't want to work in Boston which is a long way from his home in China.

D. I realize him to have a lot of talent.

E. For exercise, we usually swim in the pool that is at our health club.

F. Students who have pronunciation problems can usually get help in the language lab.

G. The travel guide tried to help the visitors who had come from foreign countries.

H. Tom was tired of traffic jams, so he decided to take the bus.

I. Because the pilot was worried about the weather, he told the passengers to buckle their seat belts.

J. _____

B

Review II: Directions
(Restrictive/Non-restrictive clauses / noun clauses / reduced adjective clauses / modifying phrases)

Read these directions and questions about the worksheet below to your partners.

2. For Sentence A, explain why we do or don't need commas.
5. Look at Sentence D. How can we correct this with a noun clause? If you need help, see Unit 7.
8. Look at Sentence E. Reduce the dependent clause to a prepositional phrase. If you need help, see Unit 20.
11. In Sentence F, did you reduce the phrase with the preposition "with"?
14. Look at Sentence H. Change this sentence so that it starts with a modifying phrase, in other words, an adjective and preposition. If you need help, see Unit 21.

Worksheet

A. The woman who won the award for "Best Actress" had graduated from my college.

B. Every Sunday, Bill buys a New York Times which is one of the most popular newspapers in the country.

C. My brother is looking for a job which will earn him a lot of money, but he doesn't want to work in Boston which is a long way from his home in China.

D. I realize him to have a lot of talent.

E. For exercise, we usually swim in the pool that is at our health club.

F. Students who have pronunciation problems can usually get help in the language lab.

G. The travel guide tried to help the visitors who had come from foreign countries.

H. Tom was tired of traffic jams, so he decided to take the bus.

I. Because the pilot was worried about the weather, he told the passengers to buckle their seat belts.

J. _____

Review II: Directions
(Restrictive/Non-restrictive clauses / noun clauses / reduced adjective clauses / modifying phrases)

Read these directions and questions about the worksheet below to your partners.

3. Look at Sentence B. Put in commas if we need them.
6. In Sentence D, did you use the word "that"?
9. Look at Sentence F. Underline the dependent clause.
12. Look at Sentence G. Underline the dependent clause.
15. Look at Sentence I. Change the sentence so that it starts with a modifying phrase, in other words, an adjecive and a prepostion. If you need help, see 21.

Worksheet

A. The woman who won the award for "Best Actress" had graduated from my college.

B. Every Sunday, Bill buys a New York Times which is one of the most popular newspapers in the country.

C. My brother is looking for a job which will earn him a lot of money, but he doesn't want to work in Boston which is a long way from his home in China.

D. I realize him to have a lot of talent.

E. For exercise, we usually swim in the pool that is at our health club.

F. Students who have pronunciation problems can usually get help in the language lab.

G. The travel guide tried to help the visitors who had come from foreign countries.

H. Tom was tired of traffic jams, so he decided to take the bus.

I. Because the pilot was worried about the weather, he told the passengers to buckle their seat belts.

J. _____

Grammar Unit 25
Common Word-Choice Problems

play and go

Examples: • They usually **play** soccer in the fall.
• To get in good physical condition, I often **go** running in the park.

Exercise 1: Match the sport with **play** or **go**.

swimming	basketball	golf	skiing	bowling
tennis	dancing	camping	skating	

We **play**: _____ _____ _____

We **go**: _____ _____ _____

_____ _____ _____

Exercise 2: For the rule below about Exercise 1, fill in the blank with **play** or **go.**

Rule: Use _____ before word-*ing* (e.g., fishing).

travel and take a trip

Exercise 3: Circle the letters of the three sentences that use the words correctly.

a. Next summer, I will **travel** to Europe.

b. Next summer, I will **trip** to Europe.

c. Next summer, I will **take a trip** to Europe.

d. We enjoyed our **trip** to Europe.

Exercise 4: For the rule below about Exercise 3, fill in the blanks with **travel** or **trip.**

Rule: _____ is a verb meaning "to go somewhere."

_____ is a noun meaning "a voyage or journey."

wish and hope

Exercise 5: (Circle) the letters of the sentences that are correct.

    a. They **hope** they **could** pass the course.

    b. They **hope** they **can** pass the course.

    c. They **wish** they **can** get their driver's license.

    d. They **wish** they **could** get their driver's license.

    e. We **hope** she **will** arrive soon.

    f. We **hope** she **would** arrive soon.

    g. We **wish** she **will** arrive soon.

    h. We **wish** she **would** arrive soon.

Exercise 6: For the rule below about Exercise 5, fill in the blanks with **wish** or **hope.**

> **Rule:** With _____, you should use **can** or **will**.
>
>   With _____, you should use **could** or **would**.

say and tell

Exercise 7: (Circle) the letters of the <u>two sentences</u> that are correct.

    a. My uncle **told** me that there was a problem.

    b. My uncle **said to** me that there was a problem.

    c. My uncle **said** me that there was a problem.

Exercise 8: Write <u>six sentences</u>. Use one of the expressions in the box below in each sentence.

• play + (a sport)	• go + (a sport)	• travel
• take a trip	• wish	• hope

_____

_____

_____

_____

_____

_____

---

even, even if, and even though

Exercise 9

❶ Read the example sentences below.
❷ For the rules in the box below, fill in the blanks with the words **even, even if,** or **even though**.

Examples:

1. He'll finish the job, <u>even if</u> he feels sick.
2. <u>Even if</u> they offered me a free trip to the moon, I wouldn't go there.

3. He passed the course <u>even though</u> he didn't study.
4. <u>Even though</u> she doesn't have a job, she is still planning to buy a car.

5. Everyone will attend the party, <u>even</u> my brother.
6. He works every day, <u>even</u> on holidays.

Rule 1   "_____" tells us that a condition will not change a future action.
It often has "will" or "would" in the independent clause.
It is similar in meaning to "**whether or not.**"

Rule 2   "_____" means the same as "**although.**"
It tells us that something really happened or is happening.

Rule 3   "_____" is used to stress the noun after it
or to stress the prepositional phrase after it.

Exercise 10

❶ Write **Right** next to the <u>three sentences</u> that are correct.
❷ Write **Wrong** next to the <u>three sentences</u> that are not correct.

_____ 1. We'll have a picnic **even** it rains.

_____ 2. We'll have a picnic **even if** it rains.

_____ 3. **Even if** she comes to my house, I will not talk to her.

_____ 4. **Even** she comes to my house, I will not talk to her.

_____ 5. He does all the housework, **even** the laundry.

_____ 6. **Even** she is sleepy, she eats breakfast every morning.

Exercise 11

Fill in the blanks with **even, even if,** or **even though.**

1. _____ he passes this course, he will not graduate.

2. _____ Tina has a driver's license, she rides her bike everywhere.

3. She enjoys every season, _____ winter.

4. Joan doesn't speak Spanish, _____ she lived in Mexico for a year.

5. _____ he loves animals, he never visits a zoo.

6. I hate snow. _____ I loved snow, I would not go skiing because I'm afraid of heights.

Exercise 12: Write two sentences with **even.**

_____

_____

Exercise 13: Write two sentences with **even if.**

_____

_____

Exercise 14: Write two sentences with **even though.**

_____

_____

Grammar Unit 26
Passive Voice

Active: My father <u>gave</u> me some money.
Passive: I <u>was</u> <u>given</u> some money by my father.

Passive:	*be*	+ **past participle**	
• He	*was*	**asked**	many questions by the reporters.
• They	*will be*	**called**	as soon as possible.
• She	*is being*	**questioned**	by the police.

Rule 1: Sentences in the <u>passive voice</u> can have "**by**," followed by someone or something. *(The "by" phrase is optional.)*

   • I was driven to the mall ***by*** *my father.* (***"by*** *my father"* is optional.)
   • Their money was stolen. (***"by*** *a thief"* is optional.)

Rule 2: If a "**by**" phrase is not possible, or doesn't make sense, use the active voice.

   mistake: I <u>was given</u> some money to my friend. *(no "**by**" phrase)*
   correct: I gave some money to my friend. *(The active form is necessary.)*

   mistake: A thief <u>was stolen</u> my money. *(It is not possible to use "**by**.")*
   correct: A thief stole my money. *(The active form is necessary.)*

Rule 3: Intransitive verbs cannot be passive voice.

   Transitive verb *(can have an object): Tech Support gives advice.*
   $$\overset{V}{\quad}\overset{obj}{\quad}$$
   Passive: *Advice is given by Tech Support.*

   Intransitive verb *(cannot have an object): The problem disappeared the next day.*
   $$\overset{V}{\quad}$$
   Mistaken Passive: *The problem <u>was</u> disappeared the next day.*
   Correct Active: *The problem <u>disappeared</u> the next day.*

Exercise 1

Write **passive** in front of the <u>four sentences</u> that are in the passive voice.

_____ 1. She was asked a question by her friend.

_____ 2. My car was repaired.

_____ 3. I am writing a letter.

_____ 4. A letter is being written by the president.

_____ 5. He was eating his dinner.

_____ 6. My car was hit.

Exercise 2

❶ Circle the object of the verb in these sentences if there is one.
❷ Identify whether the verb is transitive (with an object) or intransitive (no object).
❸ Write the transitive verb sentences in the passive.

1. They laughed during the performance. (**Note**: "performance" is an object of the preposition "during," but it is not the object of the verb, so "laugh" is an intransitive verb.)
   (Transitive/(Intransitive)) _We cannot write the sentence in the passive._

2. The earthquake killed 25 people.
   ((Transitive)/Intransitive) _Twenty-five people were killed by the earthquake._

3. The moon appeared over the horizon.
   (Transitive/Intransitive) _____

4. While running, Lee fell on the trail.
   (Transitive/Intransitive) _____

5. Our president wrote the rules for our club.
   (Transitive/Intransitive) _____

6. Their instructor taught the students the code for the new software.
   (Transitive/Intransitive) _____

7. The customers stood in line for 15 minutes.
   (Transitive/Intransitive) _____

8. Patients should take their medicine regularly.
   (Transitive/Intransitive) _____

Exercise 3

❶ Write **Right** next to the sentences that are grammatically correct. (There are five.)

❷ Write **Wrong** next to the sentences that are incorrect.

❸ If the sentence is incorrect, write it correctly.

Right 1. They were looking for the answer.

Wrong 2. She was ~~take~~ *taken* to the hospital.

_____ 3. The house was painted by the painter.

_____ 4. The boy was broken the window.

_____ 5. The phone was ringing.

_____ 6. The old man was died from a heart attack.

_____ 7. They were giving some homework by the teacher.

_____ 8. I got wet because I was fallen in the river.

_____ 9. On my birthday, I was received a new car.

_____ 10. The plane crash occurred at midnight.

_____ 11. We didn't know what was happened to our guests.

_____ 12. Next week, a music festival will held in the park.

_____ 13. A new stadium build for our football team last year.

_____ 14. The money was found under the bed.

Exercise 4

❶ Write three sentences using passive voice.

❷ (Circle) the "*be*-verb."

❸ Underline the past participle.

❹ Write **by** "someone" or **by** "something."

Example 1: That story (was) written by my brother.

Example 2: Our house (was) damaged (by the storm).

_____

_____

_____

Grammar Unit 27
Reported Speech

In formal writing, put present verbs into the past and past verbs into the past perfect.

Exercise 1

Make these statements more formal.

1. Bob said that he ~~likes~~ *liked* summer.

2. She told me that she is looking for a new roommate.

3. They said that they will start the project soon.

4. Ann said that she cannot go after work.

5. He told me that he attended school in Europe as a child.

Exercise 2

Make these questions more formal.

6. Dan asked ~~her are her classes~~ *if her classes were* difficult and ~~does she want~~ *if she wanted* to drop any of them.

7. Sue asked me can I speak a second language.

8. I asked her does she like to have coffee with breakfast.

9. Tom asked me do my friends prefer to go shopping or hiking.

Exercise 3

Make these questions more formal.

10. Jim asked what time ~~will everyone arrive~~ *everyone would arrive* for the party and where ~~do they plan~~ *they planned* to park their cars.

11. Tina wondered how can she lose weight.

12. Ted asked his friends how do they feel about cigarettes.

13. Sara wondered what does the teacher mean by "a good conclusion."

Exercise 4

In these imperative sentences, correct the underlined mistakes.

to take

14. Jim told her ~~take~~ her car to the repair shop.

15. The father told his son <u>don't</u> watch TV while eating dinner.

Exercise 5

Read this dialog.

1. ***Ann:*** I have a question that I want to ask you. How do you feel about older children who live at home after they graduate from college?

2. ***Ken:*** It depends on the situation.

3. ***Ann:*** What do you mean?

4. ***Ken:*** For example, my brother is living at home now. He finished college three months ago. He doesn't have a job, so he can't afford an apartment.

5. ***Ann:*** Are your parents upset about having the brother at home?

6. ***Ken:*** They are perhaps a little embarrassed. On the other hand, my brother is helpful, too. For example, yesterday, my brother fixed my parents' computer for them. Also, tomorrow, he will drive them to the airport, so they can avoid taking a taxi.

7. ***Ann:*** I could never live at home, because I can't get along with my father if we are together for several days. How can I improve our relationship?

8. ***Ken:*** Don't express your opinions to your father so forcefully.

9. ***Ann:*** I'll try that.

Exercise 6

Use the information from the dialog above to fill in the blanks below.

Ken saw his friend Ann the other day. . .

1. She said that _she had_ a question that she _wanted_ to ask _____ .

   She wondered _____ about older children who live at home after

   they ___graduate_____ from college.

2. He said that _____ on the situation.

3. She asked him _____.

4. He told her that, for example, _____ brother, a college graduate, _____

   _____ at home. He _____ a job, so he _____

   _____ an apartment.

5. Ann asked him _____ about having _____ brother at home.

6. Ken answered that _____ perhaps a little embarrassed. On the other hand, Ken

   added that ____ brother _____, too. For example, _____ brother

   _____ their parents' computer for them. Also, he _____ them

   to the airport, so _____ taking a taxi.

7. Ann mentioned that _____ at home, because she _____

   along with _____ father if _____ together for several days. Then she asked Ken

   _____ their relationship.

8. Ken advised her _____ her opinions to _____ father so forcefully.

9. Ann responded that _____ that.

Appendix

Guidelines and Exercises for APA Citations

When you use information in your essay that came from a source, you need to tell the reader information about that source. There are two types of citation that you do:

(1) cite the source in the body of your paper

(2) list complete source information at the end of your paper. This list at the end of the paper is often titled, "Sources Cited," "Works Cited," or "References."

Part 1: Citing sources in the body of your paper

Exercise 1

Sometimes you might paraphrase information for a source, and sometimes you might quote directly. The citation will be different when you paraphrase from when you quote.

Let's say you want to use information from this source in your essay:

(author) **James Nelson**.   (article) **"Workplace Email."**
(newspaper) *National Post*. **July 26, 2010, page 15.**

For information that you paraphrase, you can cite it like these:

Paraphrase Citation Example 1) Companies are losing millions of dollars a year because their employees are using email to send messages to friends (Nelson, 2010).

Paraphrase Citation Example 2) According to Nelson (2010), companies are losing millions of dollars a year because their employees are using email to send messages to friends.

Analysis Exercise 1: Answer the questions below about the paraphrase citation examples above.

 1. At the end of Paraphrased Citation Example 1 is "(Nelson, 2010)." What is Nelson?

    a) The last name of the student who wrote the paraphrase in the essay.

    b) The first name of the author who wrote the article that was paraphrased.

    c) The last name of the author who wrote the article that was paraphrased.

 2. What does the number "2010" refers to?

    a) It's the year that the article was in the newspaper.

    b) It's the year that the students wrote the essay.

    c) It's the page number of the article.

---

3. Why does Paraphrased Citation Example 1 have (Nelson, 2010) at the end, but Example 2 doesn't?

    a) We don't know who the author is so we don't cite one in Example 2.

    b) In Example 2, the author's last name and year are included in the opening phrase, "According to Nelson (2010)," so we don't need to repeat it at the end.

    c) It's a mistake. We should write it at the end of Example 2.

For information that you quote, you can cite it like these:

Quotation Citation Example 1) Nelson (2010) stated, "A good office manager will monitor employees' emails" (p. 28).

Quotation Citation Example 2) The article reports, "Secretly reading employees' emails could cause problems" (Nelson, 2010, p. 30).

Analysis Exercise 2: Answer the questions below about the quotation citations examples above.

4. What are (**p. 28**) and (**p. 30**) in these Quotation Citation Examples?

    a) It tells the reader what page of the newspaper that the quotation came from.

    b) It tells the reader how many page the article was.

    c) It tells the reader how many pages the student's essay is.

5. Question 5: Quotation Citation Example 1 has only **Nelson (2010)** but Example 4 has (**Nelson, 2010, p. 30**). Why are these different?

    a) It's a mistake. We should write the (2010, p. 30) in Example 1.

    b) The student who wrote this wants the reader to notice the page number in Example 1 but not in Example 2.

    c) In Example 1, the author's last name and year are included in the opening phrase, "According to Nelson (2010)," so we don't' need to repeat it at the end. We just need to write the page number where the quote came from.

Exercise 3: The book source for the information below is

    (author) **Tom Wilson.**   (book) **Testing Reading.**

    (city, publisher, year) **New York: Lowman, 2005**, (page of quotation) **p. 70.**

Write the correct information in the parenthesis ( ) below.

1. As Americans read less for fun, their reading scores are declining (   ).
2. According to Wilson (   ), fewer than half of Americans over 18 read novels.
3. Students who lived at home where there were more than 100 books performed better on tests than ones who lived in homes with fewer books (   ).
4. Wilson (   ) argues, "Students who read for fun every day perform better on reading tests than those who don't" (   )
5. The author points out, "Nearly 90% of employers rated reading comprehension as very important for workers" (   )

Part 2: Listing complete "Sources Cited" information <u>at the end of your paper</u>

Book:

    Last name, First name initial. (Year Published). *Book Title*. City, State: Publisher.

Example:

    Mischel, W. (2014). *The Marshmallow Test*. New York, N.Y.: Little, Brown.

Magazine:

    Last name, First name initial. (Year, Month Date Published). Article title. *Magazine Title*, Page(s).

Example:

    Trudeau, Garry. (2010, October). The story of a generation. *The Atlantic*, 74-77.

Journal:

    Last name, First name initial. (Year Published). Article title. *Journal Title*, Volume (Issue), Page(s).

Example: (Note: In this example, there are two authors.)

    Carson, J. & Nelson, G.. (1994). Writing Groups: Cross-Cultural Issues. *Journal of Second Language Writing* (3), 17-30.

Website:

Last name, First name initial. (Year, Month Date Published). *Webpage title*. Retrieved from URL

Example:

Smith, P. (2017, August 22). *Why You Feel So Stressed Out After A Vacation*. Retrieved from http://www.huffingtonpost.com/entry/post-vacation-stressblues_us_5995dd4ee4b0a2608a6a96dc

Exercise 4. Imagine that you used information from these three sources in your essay. At the end of your essay, you will write "Sources Cited." Write these in the correct citation form. (You can underline the book / magazine title.)

1. **Book**: The Lives of Apes. Publisher: Seligman. City: Chicago. Author: Jane Goodwin. Year: 1998.

2. **Magazine:** Sports Illustrated. Author: Steve Kroff. Article: The Summer Olympics. Date: April 7, 2007. pages 28-30.

3. **Book with two authors:** Publisher: Peguin. Authors: Bill Timms and Donna Reep. Year: 2004. Book title: Child Wisdom. City: Seattle.

Other books from Pro Lingua
AT THE INTERMEDIATE AND ADVANCED LEVELS

Also by David and Peggy Kehe

- **Writing Strategies, Book One – Intermediate**— The first book of *Writing Strategies* covers the following essay types: Description, Process, Narration, Cause and Effect, Exposition, Extended Definition, Comparison and Contrast, Argumentation,' and Expository Essay with a Source.

- **Write after Input** — Entertaining student-centered activities to lead the low-intermediate learner inductively to better writing. **The five units** guide students from constructing a single paragraph in **Unit One,** to two and more paragraphs in **Units 2-4** and finally, to a five-paragraph composition in **Unit 5.**

- **Basic Conversation Strategies** — Structured pair and small group activities for developing strategic conversation skills at the high-beginning, low-intermediate level with a focus on training the learners to be good listeners. The teachers edition includes the student edition and scripts of the listening activities, and notes and suggestions to the teacher. Two CDs have 67 listening exercises.

- **Conversation Strategies** — 29 structured pair activities for developing strategic conversation skills at the intermediate level. Students learn the words, phrases, and conventions used by native speakers in active, give-and-take, everyday conversation.

- **Discussion Strategies** — Carefully structured pair and small group work at the advanced-intermediate level. Excellent preparation for students who will participate in academic or professional work that requires effective participation in discussion and seminars.

- **The Grammar Review Book** — This easy-to-use book is designed for anyone who has learned English by ear and who needs to write grammatically. The students learn to recognize and correct common, fossilized errors through a carefully sequenced series of exercises.

- **Cultural Differences** — A content-based college/university preparation course introducing and giving practice in using a wide range of academic skills. It is of value to English language learners and native speakers who are or will be living in a culturally diverse environment and community. The content is focused on a neglected area of language-culture studies: the confusion, misunderstandings, misconceptions, and sometimes even hostilities that can occur when learners don't really understand each other's language and culture.

Shenanigames — Grammar-focused, interactive ESL activities and games providing practice with a full range of grammar structures. Photocopyable.

Getting a Fix on Vocabulary — A student text and workbook that focuses on affixation—building words by adding prefixes and suffixes to a root.